Ready-to-Use
Activities for
Teaching
ROMEO

&
JULIET

Ready-to-Use Activities for Teaching ROMEO & JULIET

JOHN WILSON SWOPE

THE CENTER FOR APPLIED
RESEARCH IN EDUCATION

Library of Congress Cataloging-in-Publication Data

Swope, John Wilson.
    Ready-to-use activities for teaching Romeo and Juliet / by John
Wilson Swope.
        p.   cm. — (Shakespeare teacher's activities library)
    Includes bibliographical references.
    ISBN 0-87628-114-5
    1. Shakespeare, William, 1564-1616.   Romeo and Juliet.
2. Shakespeare, William, 1564-1616—Study and teaching (Secondary)
3. Activity programs in education.   I. Title.   II. Series.
PR2831.S94   1993
822.3'3—dc20   93-13964
                                                                       CIP

ISBN 0-87628-114-5

THE CENTER FOR APPLIED RESEARCH
IN EDUCATION

On the World Wide Web at http://www.phdirect.com

Printed in the United States of America

Dedication

To my wife, friend, and colleague:
Mary Jo P. Wagner

John Wilson Swope

In addition to eleven years as a middle and secondary English, speech, and drama teacher, John Wilson Swope has taught English education courses at the University of Florida and the University of Northern Iowa, where he is currently an assistant professor of English. His articles and reviews have appeared in *English Journal, English Leadership Quarterly, FOCUS, The Leaflet,* and *The Virginia English Bulletin.* He is a frequent presenter at conferences sponsored by the National Council of Teachers in English and its local affiliates. As an actor, director, and designer, he has participated in more than a dozen community theater productions.

About This Resource

Shakespeare's *Romeo and Juliet*, like *Julius Caesar*, *Hamlet*, and *Macbeth*, is a common choice among literature programs. As teachers, we enjoy these works and think them important for more than their stories. For me, Shakespeare's ability to observe human nature and convey it through language commands my attention. His characters act and interact with others in ways that I recognize around me. His poetry conveys human experience through timeless literary form.

Although we prize Shakespeare's plays, they present many problems for our students as first-time readers. As teachers, we want our students to comprehend the plot, understand the motives of the characters, appreciate the language, and decipher countless allusions—sometimes after only a single reading.

For many students, *Romeo and Juliet* is an introduction to Shakespeare's plays. These students aren't expert in Elizabethan language or conventions of blank verse; however, they possess knowledge and personal experience to help them understand and appreciate the play. Chronologically, they are between thirteen and seventeen, the ages of Juliet and Romeo. They have friends of whom their parents disapprove. They know the whimsical nature of teenage love and may believe, as Shakespeare's young lovers do, that fate brings them together. And, like Romeo and Juliet, they may solve their problems impulsively rather than rationally. When we help students recall, organize, and share their relevant knowledge and experience, it becomes a valuable resource for them to begin understanding, appreciating, and interpreting the play.

As with other volumes in the *Shakespeare Teacher's Activities Library*, *Ready-to-Use Materials for Teaching Romeo and Juliet* is a collection of student-centered activities for presenting the play to first-time readers. I've designed these activities to help students recall prior knowledge and personal experience that they can relate to the play. When students have little prior knowledge or experience that they can relate to the play, I have designed activities—like the plot summaries, scenarios for improvisation, or prereading vocabulary—to create or enhance their knowledge.

Although students expect structure in a classroom, they tend to dislike a single routine. This resource presents choices of activities to help students make connections between their lives and Shakespeare's *Romeo and Juliet*. The activities afford students opportunities to read, write, think, speak, and act out in response to the play.

In developing these activities, I've drawn upon research in effective teaching, reading, whole language, and English education as well as my experience as a classroom teacher. I have also had the opportunities to team teach with my friends and colleagues, Sue Ellen Savereide, instructor at the Malcolm Price Laboratory School, Cedar Falls, Iowa, and Sharon Palas, English teacher at Denver High School, Denver, Iowa, in developing these materials.

Although these activities will help get your students involved with *Romeo and Juliet*, I don't propose that these are the only ones that work with students. As the teacher, you determine which activities the students use, and whether they work individually, in pairs, small groups, or as a whole class. You also need to decide whether the students read silently, aloud, or in combination. I also encourage you to continue using the films and professional recordings of the play that have worked in the past, for both films and recordings may be used as prereading, reading, or postreading techniques. In addition to the ideas I present here, I urge you to develop your own specific improvisations, questions, and extending activities that reflect your specific teaching objectives and best fit your district's curriculum.

John Wilson Swope

Table of Contents

During-Reading Activities

Postreading Activities

PROLOGUE AND ACT II

Focusing Activities

Prereading Activities

During-Reading Activities

ACT III

ACT IV

ACT V

During-Reading Activities

Postreading Activities

Extending Activities

PART THREE: APPENDICES

PART ONE

Suggestions to the Teacher

READING PROCESSES

RATIONALE

ORGANIZATION OF ACTIVITIES

PREREADING ACTIVITIES

DURING-READING ACTIVITIES

POSTREADING ACTIVITIES

EXTENDING ACTIVITIES

SUMMARY OF READING PROCESS
    ACTIVITIES FOR *ROMEO AND JULIET*

A Guide to Using This Resource

READING PROCESSES

In recent years, teachers have come to teach writing as a process of prewriting, writing, and rewriting. Approaching reading as a similar process of prereading, during reading, and postreading allows students to approach difficult texts systematically, enhancing their comprehension, understanding, and appreciation. As a linguistic process, effective reading involves the reader: the reader anticipates what the text may reveal, reads to confirm or contradict those goals, and then thinks about what has been read.

To guide you in using reading as a process to teach *Romeo and Juliet,* this section will

- explain reading processes,
- establish a rationale for using reading as a process in studying the play,
- explain the overall organization of the student activities, and
- explain the function of each of the activities in this resource.

All activities follow a reading processes model and fall into the following three major groups, with a fourth group of optional activities called *extending activities.*

Prereading activities help students assess and organize information or personal experience that relates to what they will read. These activities help students to connect their prior knowledge to the text as well as help them to establish a genuine purpose for reading it.

During-reading activities encourage students to read actively rather than passively, taking more responsibility for their own learning. Because full comprehension of a text doesn't occur immediately upon reading it the first time, students often need help to make sense of what they've just read. By structuring reading sessions and using reading, writing, speaking, listening, viewing, and critical thinking activities to foster active contemplation of the text, students can begin to explore their possible interpretations of the text.

Postreading activities help students make sense of their earlier explorations of the literature and come to an overall understanding of a work.

Extending activities allow students to apply what they've learned about the text to new situations after they've reached an understanding of the work.

RATIONALE

Reading *Romeo and Juliet* is difficult, even for the most proficient students. As teachers, when we read the play along with our students, we may be reading the text for the tenth or twentieth time. We may forget that our students are encountering this text for the first time. As teachers and students of literature ourselves, we have developed our appreciation, understanding, interpretations, and love of Shakespeare's plays through our repeated exposure to them. We have read, reread, contemplated, researched, discussed, listened to, and viewed performances of them. The activities in this resource apply a reading process approach to the study of *Romeo and Juliet* and encourage students to read, reread, contemplate, discuss, listen to, and view the play as active readers and learners, enhancing their understanding, appreciation, and enjoyment of it.

This resource provides you with choices of activities to help students understand *Romeo and Juliet*. The selection of activities depends upon the students you teach, your instructional goals, and the time you wish to devote to the study of the play. For example, a unit using these materials would include

- 🙠 completing one focusing activity and reviewing the plot summary for a specific scene as a prereading activity,

- 🙠 keeping either a character diary or a response journal throughout the reading of the play as a during-reading activity,

- 🙠 completing one of the postreading activities.

The vocabulary, viewing a scene on videotape, guides to character development, critical thinking questions, language exploration, and extending activities are other options to achieve additional instructional goals.

ORGANIZATION OF ACTIVITIES

To facilitate the planning of your unit, I've grouped the students' activities according to act. For each act, I've arranged the activities according to the stage of the reading process—prereading, during-reading, postreading. (See Figure 1: Summary of Reading Process Activities for *Romeo and Juliet* located at the end of Part One). Extending activities, designed for use only after a complete reading of the play, follow the materials for Act V. Answer keys for quizzes and suggested answers for discussion activities are located in appendices.

PREREADING ACTIVITIES

The prereading activities for *Romeo and Juliet* include focusing activities, plot summaries, and vocabulary.

Focusing Activities

All focusing activities share a common goal: to help students organize and apply relevant prior knowledge and experience to the scene they are about to read. Because they set the stage for reading, they should be brief, generally between five and ten minutes. These activities help establish a genuine purpose for reading by encouraging students to speculate about what *may* happen rather than to predict accurately what *does happen* in the play. Although several different focusing activities are available for each scene of the play, students need to complete *only one* of them:

scenarios for improvisation, prereading discussion questions, speculation journal, or introducing the play with videotape.

Scenarios for Improvisation. These improvisational group activities take a few minutes for students to prepare and present but allow them to explore possible motives and actions of characters in situations that relate to a particular scene. Once they present an improvisation to the class, it becomes a common experience and a part of each person's relevant prior knowledge. A brief discussion of the improvisation will help connect the improvisation to the action of the play. After reading, the students may wish to discuss the similarities between the improvisation and what actually happened in the scene.

Prereading Discussion Questions. As an anticipatory device, these questions allow students to talk through their speculations about what they will read. The questions tend to be more effective once everyone has become familiar with a play and its characters.

Speculation Journal. This activity begins as an individual writing-to-learn activity. After students speculate for three to five minutes about what *might* happen, encourage them to share their predictions. Keep in mind that the goal is for them to use what they know about characters and motivations, to explore what logically *could* happen and not to guess correctly what *does* happen.

Introducing the Play with Videotape. Showing the opening scenes of a play before students begin reading it can be an excellent introductory focusing activity. A visual presentation provides them with a sense of the setting and overall action of the scene before they confront the written text. After showing the film or tape, ask the class, "What seems to be going on here?" A few minutes' discussion will help you determine if the class has a general sense of what they've seen.

Plot Summaries

Once students have completed a focusing activity, share the plot summary of the scene with them before they begin reading it. Reading the summary helps students establish the overall direction for the scene before beginning Shakespeare's verse. With the summary as a road map, students are less likely to get lost among Shakespeare's many literary allusions.

Vocabulary

The vocabulary activities allow students to expand their vocabularies through repeated exposure to words within context. The words defined in the prereading lists are the bases for both of the postreading vocabulary activities: vocabulary in context and vocabulary review quiz. Although most of the words on these lists are in common use today, Shakespeare often used them in different contexts than contemporary speakers do. The lists provide brief definitions and synonyms as well as a sentence to illustrate the word in a context similar to the one the students will encounter in the play.

DURING-READING ACTIVITIES

Students need to read actively. When the text is as challenging as *Romeo and Juliet*, few students can comprehend it immediately. Instead, most of them need to contemplate the text consciously to make sense of it. During-reading activities allow them to reread, write, talk, listen, view, and think about what they've just read.

Four types of activities enable students to contemplate actively what they've just read and begin to explore possible interpretations of it: *response journal, character diary, viewing scenes on videotape,* and *guides to character development.*

Response Journal

This writing-to-learn activity is based upon the work of David Bleich. The students make four types of responses either while they read or immediately upon completing the reading of a particular scene. They respond emotionally to what they're reading and try to speculate why the text provokes a particular response. Then they record and explore their own associations and experiences that relate to the text. The figurative response then draws the students back to the text, making them contemplate an important section of it. Finally, the response journal encourages students to record the questions that arise while they read, so they can address them later.

All students keep an individual response journal throughout their reading of *Romeo and Juliet.* They can use it as a means to record their reactions to what they read either while they read or immediately upon completing a reading session. For example, if students read the play aloud during class, encourage them to take the last few minutes of the period to write in their response journals. If students are to read outside of class, then also have them complete their response journals as part of the homework assignment. The writing in the response journal is exploratory in nature: it is a forum for formulating and testing hypotheses about the play, its language, and its characters; it is not a place where grammar, usage, and mechanics are an issue.

Character Diary

An alternative to the response journal, this exploratory writing-to-learn activity encourages students to read actively and to contemplate what they've read. The students summarize the action of the play, in the form of a personal diary, from the perspective of a minor character. Because no character is present for all the action of a play, the character diary requires students to provide a logical account of how their individual character comes to know the action. This paraphrasing not only improves students' reading comprehension but affects a broad range of related language skills, "including literal recall of events, characters, main points, rhetorical features, stylistic devices and text structure" (Brown and Cambourne, 9). Like the response journal, the writing in the character diary is exploratory in nature.

Viewing a Scene on Videotape

As an optional during-reading activity, students view and discuss several scenes immediately after having read them. These include Romeo and Juliet's meeting (Act I, scene v), the first balcony scene (Act II, scene ii), the second balcony scene (Act III, scene v), and Juliet's chance meeting with Paris when she goes to Friar Laurence for help (Act IV, scene i).

Because the students will already be familiar with the play's language, action, and characters, viewing the scene permits them to use the additional visual and auditory information to improve their understanding of the play's language and characters. For example, seeing professional actors portray Romeo and Juliet's first meeting demonstrates the verbal game of courtly love that both Romeo and Juliet play well. Similarly, viewing the first and second balcony scenes helps to examine the changes in Romeo's and Juliet's characters.

Guides to Character Development

These guides are additional, optional means to structure the students' contemplation of a play. Four sets of guides to character development and revelation include Romeo and Juliet as major characters and Mercutio and the Nurse as minor ones.

How you use these activities depends on the specific goals for studying *Romeo and Juliet*. For example, you can have the entire class examine how Shakespeare develops a major character by having them choose to examine either Romeo or Juliet. Similarly, they may examine how Shakespeare reveals minor, and more static characters like Mercutio or the Nurse. Have them complete these activities individually, in pairs, or in small groups.

These charts direct students first to review specific portions of the play to determine what characters do, say, or what other characters say about them before drawing conclusions about what insight this information provides into a specific character. You will find charts for the characters with the during-reading materials for each act in which the specific character appears. Juliet appears in all five acts, Romeo in all but Act IV, the Nurse in all but Act V, and Mercutio appears only in the first three.

POSTREADING ACTIVITIES

Postreading activities help students read, write, talk, or act their ways through the play to reach an overall understanding of it. This resource provides four types of postreading activities: *comprehension checks, critical thinking questions, language exploration,* and *vocabulary.*

Comprehension Checks

Two types of activities assess students' comprehension of the text that they've read: a multiple choice quiz and small group discussion questions.

Comprehension Check (multiple choice). The quizzes consist of five multiple choice questions for each act. Two are factual, two are interpretative, and one is evaluative.

Small Group Discussion Questions to Check Comprehension. These questions help students assess whether they understand key issues of a play. Encourage them to discuss their answers with one another and return to the text to clarify misunderstandings through collaborative discussion in small groups.

Critical Thinking Questions

Postreading discussion questions are probably the most common activity in a literature classroom. However, questions need to do more than simply check whether the students have read a particular passage. The Critical Thinking Questions follow the model of Christenbury and Kelly and help students connect the act that they've just read with the play as a whole, to their personal experiences, and to other literary experiences. To establish the goal for the discussion, present the focus question first. Although this question is the one that students will find difficult to answer at first, present it to them and just let them think about it. Explore the related issues in the other questions and then have the students return to the focus question to connect their other responses to it.

Language Exploration

These activities allow students to return to the text and explore how Shakespeare uses language within the context of the acts of the play that they've already read. You can encourage them to use these activities to review and apply concepts and to develop interpretations of specific passages. The concepts in *Romeo and Juliet* include changed sentence order, an introduction to figurative language and simile, metaphor, personification, and apostrophe.

Vocabulary Activities

Vocabulary in Context. For a postreading activity, students can examine how Shakespeare uses the prereading vocabulary within a specific passage. Then, the students can apply an appropriate meaning and develop an interpretation of the passage within the context of the play. Although these activities direct students to excerpts, you can encourage students to review an entire section of the particular scene to establish a more complete context.

Vocabulary Review Quizzes. These activities provide students with ways to assess their mastery of vocabulary for each act. The quiz items deliberately repeat, in modern language, the context established in the vocabulary in context activities. These quizzes are in a multiple choice format to facilitate evaluation.

EXTENDING ACTIVITIES

Extending activities encourage students to apply what they've learned from studying *Romeo and Juliet* to alternative situations. Students may complete these activities individually or in groups. This resource includes general directions for extending activities as well as more specific directions for acting out, oral interpretation, using puppet theater, making masks, and writing assignments.

Acting Out

Through improvisations, students can work out a skit to portray a particular scene or place a familiar character in a different context.

Oral Interpretation

These activities encourage students to present scenes from the play in its original language. With the suggested scenes, students can work either individually or in pairs. The directions include steps for preparing an effective oral interpretation. Students may wish to incorporate either puppet theater or masks into their presentations.

Puppet Theater

This activity includes directions for making paper bag puppets and suggestions for two, three, or more performers for specific scenes.

Paper Plate Masks

Masks provide a way to present visual interpretations of a character. Students can do this easily by constructing simple masks from paper plates as shown. These masks, like the puppets, may also be combined with oral or dramatic presentations.

Writing Assignments

Writing tasks give students a chance to incorporate their new understanding of the play into a piece of writing. To develop these assignments, they may want to use some of their reading process activities, such as response journals or character diaries, as sources for prewriting.

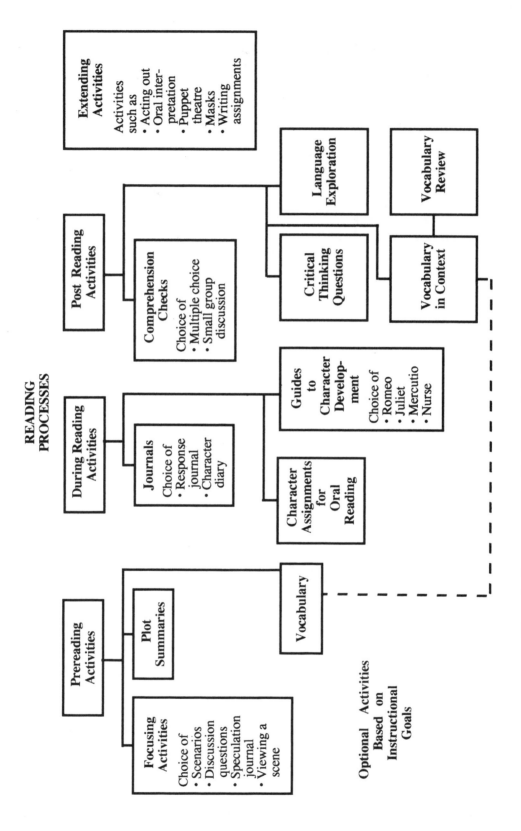

READING
PROCESSES

Extending Activities

Activities such as
• Acting out
• Oral inter-
  pretation
• Puppet
  theatre
• Masks
• Writing
  assignments

Language Exploration

Vocabulary Review

Post Reading Activities

Comprehension Checks

Choice of
• Multiple choice
• Small group
  discussion

Critical Thinking Questions

Vocabulary in Context

During Reading Activities

Journals

Choice of
• Response
  journal
• Character
  diary

Guides to Character Develop- ment

Choice of
• Romeo
• Juliet
• Mercutio
• Nurse

Character Assignments for Oral Reading

Prereading Activities

Plot Summaries

Vocabulary

Focusing Activities

Choice of
• Scenarios
• Discussion
  questions
• Speculation
  journal
• Viewing a
  scene

Optional Activities
Based on
Instructional
Goals

Figure 1: Summary of Reading Process Activities for Romeo and Juliet

PART TWO

Ready-to-Use Materials for the Student

INTRODUCTORY MATERIALS
FOR
TEACHING SHAKESPEARE

William Shakespeare

William Shakespeare
April 23, 1564–April 23, 1616

William Shakespeare was the eldest son and third child of John Shakespeare and Mary Arden. His father was a maker of white leather (whittawer) and gloves (glover), and was a wool dealer as well as yeoman farmer who owned his own land. As a prosperous and respected tradesman, John Shakespeare also took part in the local government of Stratford and held several government positions including Chamberlain (town treasurer), Alderman (town councilman), and Bailiff of Stratford-upon-Avon.

During William's childhood, Stratford was a prosperous, self-governing market town. As a result, the Corporation of Stratford maintained the grammar school founded originally by the medieval Gild of the Holy Cross. Here historians believe young William received his early education.

The school's gildhall was also where traveling companies of actors probably performed. Records of the town suggest that William could have seen his first plays during his boyhood. The Chamberlain's accounts show that different companies of traveling players appeared and were paid from the borough's accounts on more than thirty occasions.

Town and church documents also show that William Shakespeare married Ann Hathaway when he was eighteen and she was twenty-six in 1582. They had three children, Susanna (1583) and twins Hamnet (1585–96) and Judith (1585–1662).

Shortly after his children were born, Shakespeare left Stratford and nothing is known of his life until he began acting in London in 1592. In London, he acted and served as a reviser and writer of plays. At age twenty-eight, he began to impress his contemporaries with the quality and popularity of his work. He published his first narrative poem, *Venus and Adonis* in 1593 and *The Rape of Lucrece* the following year.

While living in London, Shakespeare acted with several companies including the Chamberlain's Men (later called the King's Men) who provided entertainment for the Royal Court. He wrote many of his plays for his own acting company. Shakespeare was also partner in several theatrical ventures including being one of the proprietors of the Globe theater that was built just outside the city limits of London in 1599. His partners in the Globe also included the famous actors of the time—Richard Burbage, Will Kempe, John Heminge, and Henry Condell. Heminge and Condell would publish the first collected editions of Shakespeare's plays, known as the First Folio, in 1623.

Although Shakespeare continued to live and work in London until 1610, he purchased New Place, one of the largest houses in Stratford, in 1597. When he retired to New Place in 1610, he was a wealthy landowner whose estate included farmland, pasture, and gardens. Making occasional visits to London until 1614, Shakespeare continued to associate with actors and playwrights for the rest of his life. While in retirement at Stratford, he surrounded himself with family and friends.

Shakespeare died at home on April 23, St. George's, Day in 1616. He was buried in the chancel of Holy Trinity Church in Stratford. He willed New Place to his elder daughter Susanna, then wife of Dr. John Hall. Shakespeare's widow probably lived there with the Halls until her death in 1623. Within a few years of Shakespeare's death, a monument to him was erected and placed on the north wall of Westminster Abbey in London.

An Introduction to Shakespeare's Language

Because Shakespeare wrote nearly four hundred years ago, some of the conventions that he uses in his plays present problems for modern readers. Most of Shakespeare's lines are written in poetry. Although these lines don't usually rhyme, they do have a set rhythm (called *meter*). To achieve the meter, Shakespeare arranges words so that the syllables, which are stressed or said more loudly than others, fall in a regular pattern: dah DUM dah DUM dah DUM dah DUM dah DUM. For example, read the following lines from *Romeo and Juliet* aloud:

&

Good pilgrim, you do wrong your hand too much,
Which mannerly devotion shows in this.(I,v)

&

Because you are familiar with the words that Shakespeare uses here, you naturally stressed every second syllable:

&

Good PIL'grim, YOU' do WRONG' your HAND' too MUCH',
Which MAN'nerLY' deVO'tion SHOWS' in THIS'.

&

The pattern of one unstressed syllable followed by a stressed one, dah DUM, is called an *iamb*. Each pattern is referred to as a *foot*. Because Shakespeare uses five iambic feet to a line, this pattern in known as *iambic pentameter*.

In order for Shakespeare to maintain the set meter of most lines, he often structures the lines differently than normal English speech. He may change the normal order of words so that the stressed syllables fall in the appropriate place. For example, the following sentence has no set meter:

&

This MORN'ing BRINGS' WITH' it a GLOOM'ing PEACE'.

&

However, Shakespeare turns these words around a bit to maintain the meter in *Romeo and Juliet:*

&

a GLOOM'ing PEACE' this MORN'ing WITH' it BRINGS'.

&

He may also shorten words by omitting letters so that a two-syllable word is one syllable. As a result, *over* often appears as *o'er* and *'tis* in place of *it is*.

Shakespeare also uses forms of words that we rarely use today, four hundred years later. Among these are the personal pronouns *thou* (you), *thine* (your, yours), *thee* (you as in "to you"), and *thyself* (yourself). Often Shakespeare also uses verb endings that we no longer use. For example, *hath* is an old form of *has* and *art* an older form of *are*. You're also likely to encounter several words or phrases that we no longer use at all: *anon* instead of *soon* or *shortly* or *prithee* meaning *I pray to thee (you)*.

17

Conventions of Shakespeare's Staging

When we attend theatrical performances—school plays, assembly programs, or movies in public theaters—we're accustomed to finding a seat and waiting until the lights dim, the audience quiets down, and the play or feature begins. We're also used to seeing scenery that suggests the location of the play and expect the stage lighting to help set the mood.

But all this was not so in Shakespeare's time. Then people attended plays during the day, for there was no way to light the stage effectively once the sun had set. Public performance of plays in theaters was a fairly new idea at the time because the first permanent English theater had been built less than twenty years before Shakespeare began writing his plays. Although the shape of the theaters varied from square, circular, or octagon, all had a stage that was simply a raised platform in an open yard surrounded with tiers of galleries to accommodate the spectators. The stage was covered with a roof, commonly called "The Heavens." While the roof protected the actors from the weather, the attic space above could hold machinery, such as ropes and pulleys to lower thrones or heavenly deities to the stage or to hide the sound effects of thunder, alarum bells, or cannonades. By modern standards these theaters were small. The open yard in front of the stage in one theater measured only fifty-five feet across. Up to two thousand spectators could either sit on benches in the tiers of galleries or stand in the open yard in front of the stage.

These theaters used simple stage props—chairs or tables were brought on the raised platform as needed. Actual scenery may have been suggested through dialogue or may have included minimal set pieces such as a few trees to suggest a forest, or a rock to suggest a river bank. The stages themselves had many built-in acting areas that could function in a number of ways: for instance, small inner stages with drapes which the actors used as inner rooms or raised balconies. The actors could use the inner room for King Duncan's chamber in *Macbeth* or Brutus' tent in *Julius Caesar*. The balcony might serve as Juliet's balcony in *Romeo and Juliet* or as the battlements of Elsinore Castle in *Hamlet*.

The costumes were based on the contemporary clothing styles of the time. Instead of attempting any sort of accurate historical costuming, the actors wore clothes much like those of a character's rank. For example, Macbeth would have been costumed as any nobleman and Lady Capulet as any wealthy English merchant's wife. Occasionally, other costume pieces may have been added to suggest witches, fairies, national or racial costumes.

During the time that Shakespeare wrote and acted, only three or four professional companies performed in theaters just outside the limits of London. These professional troupes employed only male actors. Although most of the roles in Shakespeare's plays are male, the few parts of younger female characters—Juliet or her mother, for instance—were played by young boys, aged fourteen or so and apprenticed to actors. Men may have played some female roles, especially those of older, comedic women, such as Juliet's Nurse.

© 1993 by The Center for Applied Research in Education

18

PRINCIPAL CITIES FOR
ROMEO AND JULIET

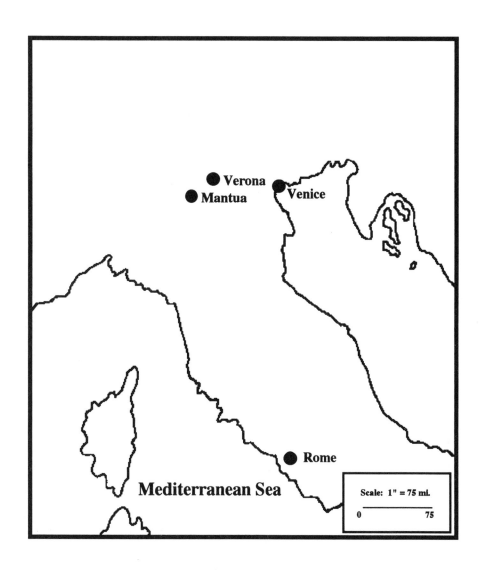

PROLOGUE
AND
ACT I

NAME:_____ DATE:_____

Focusing Activities
for
Romeo and Juliet
Scenarios for Improvisation
Act I

Directions: Presented below are locations and situations involving characters. Before reading an individual scene, pretend to be one of the characters and act out the situation. Don't worry about speaking like characters in Shakespeare's play; just try to imagine how you would react to the situation and use your own language. Take a few minutes to discuss with the other performers what you would like to do. Be prepared to act out your scene for others in the class. Afterward, classmates outside your group may discuss what they've seen.

scene i. *Scene:* The school cafeteria or commons area before school, at lunch, or immediately after school.

Characters: Pat and Leslie, Jamie and Kim.

Situation: Pat and Leslie are good friends and hold a grudge against Jamie and Kim. Pat and Leslie see the other two and want to provoke a fight. Pat and Leslie want to make it seem to the administrators or teachers in the area that Jamie and Kim started the fight.

scene ii. *Scene:* Capulet's business.

Characters: Paris, a young attorney and Lord Capulet, a wealthy merchant.

Situation: Paris, a wealthy young man with good family background and stable income, wishes to marry Lord Capulet's daughter, Juliet. Juliet, who will turn fourteen in a few weeks, is the Capulets' only surviving child. Improvise the conversation between Paris and Lord Capulet.

scene iii. *Scene:* Juliet's room.

Characters: Juliet, Lady Capulet (her mother).

Situation: Juliet's mother wants her daughter to marry a wealthy, slightly older man, Paris. Juliet, who will turn fourteen in a few weeks, is the Capulets' only surviving child. Improvise the conversation between them.

23

NAME:_____   DATE:_____

© 1993 by The Center for Applied Research in Education

Focusing Activities
for
Romeo and Juliet
Small Group Discussion Questions
Prologue and Act I

Directions: Before reading scenes in Act I, discuss the questions in small groups. You may want to make notes about your discussion so you can share them with classmates or refer back to them after you've read the scene.

scene i.

1. Based upon what you may have heard or seen, what do you think happens in the play, *Romeo and Juliet*?

2. Suppose you are the ruler of a small kingdom and have absolute control over the lives of your subjects. In recent weeks, rival gangs have fought in the streets several times, destroying property and killing innocent people and gang members. What might you do to prevent these fights from erupting again?

scene ii.

1. If you were a wealthy man, how would you respond when the Prince's cousin asked your permission to marry your 14-year-old daughter, who is your only child?

2. Suppose you couldn't read. Your boss gives you a list of things to do before you go home for the day. Knowing your job depends upon completing all the items on the list, how would you find out what they are?

scene iii. If you were Juliet's mother, how would you break the news to your daughter that a wealthy cousin of the local Prince wants to marry her? Whom might you get to help you? What do you suppose Juliet would reply?

scene iv.

1. If you were Romeo, about to crash a party at your sworn enemy's home, how would you act?

2. If you were Romeo's friend and knew that Romeo was going to crash the Capulets' party because Rosaline, his latest love, was to be there, how would you treat him?

scene v.

1. How do you think Tybalt would react if he recognized Romeo at the banquet?

2. What do you think would happen at the banquet?

Focusing Activities
for
Romeo and Juliet
Speculation Journal
Act I

Directions: This activity will help you become involved actively with reading the play by helping you to determine a definite purpose for reading. Before you read these scenes in Act I, take a few minutes to respond in writing to the questions below. Don't worry about correct answers here. Use your own experience or what you have read in the play to speculate about what you think will happen. Sometimes, as for scenes i through v below, you may be asked to speculate about issues that parallel the action of the play. After reading a scene you may find that characters reacted differently than you thought. Don't worry about these differences; just make note of them because you will have opportunities to share these differences in other activities.

Prologue and scene i. Based upon what you have seen or heard, what do you expect *Romeo and Juliet* to be about?

scene ii. If you were Lord Capulet, how would you feel about your 14-year-old daughter marrying a cousin of the Prince?

scenes iii and iv. If you were a boy of 17 or a girl of almost 14, how might you feel about falling in love? What might you think about marriage?

scene v. Romeo and his friends crash the Capulets' party thinking that they will have an opportunity to see Rosaline. Because the title of the play is *Romeo and Juliet,* what do you think will happen at the party?

26

Romeo and Juliet: Act I Speculation Journal (continued)

After Reading Act I: Now that you have finished reading the act, compare your speculations with the action of the act. Which of your speculations were most accurate? How do you account for them? Which ones were least like the action of the play? Why do you think you speculated as you did?

NAME:_____ DATE:_____

Focusing Activity
for
Romeo and Juliet
Introducing the Play with Videotape

Directions: Before you begin reading *Romeo and Juliet*, you will view a video version of the first two scenes. Don't worry about trying to understand everything, just go for general impressions. Note any questions you may want to ask your teacher afterwards. After viewing the scene, take a few minutes to respond to the questions below.

1. In your own words, describe what you saw briefly. What seems to be the overall conflict or problem?

2. Where does the scene take place? Which particular details help you to understand the action?

3. What kinds of things can the director of the film or video version do to depict the street fight and its resolution that a director could not do in a production of a stage play?

© 1993 by The Center for Applied Research in Education

NAME:_____   DATE:_____

Prereading Activity
for
Romeo and Juliet
Vocabulary
Act I

Directions: Shakespeare uses the following words in Act I. The section below provides a brief definition of each word and provides a sentence to illustrate its meaning.

Definitions.

scene i

1. **augment:** (v.) to increase or intensify.
   Example: During a recording session, the sound engineer may use special effects to *augment* the quality of a singer's voice on the album.

2. **adversary:** (n.) opponent, foe, enemy.
   Example: The other high school in the county has always been our chief *adversary* in the district football championship.

3. **chaste:** (adj.) virtuous, decent, pure in style or manner, virginal.
   Example: Both Rosaline and Juliet behave in a *chaste* manner.

4. **exquisite:** (adj.) of special beauty or charm.
   Example: The engagement ring, set with a small, blue sapphire surrounded with diamonds, was *exquisite*.

5. **forfeit:** (n.) fine, penalty. (v.) to lose or be liable to lose as a result of a crime.
   Example: Noah found the *forfeit* of his reckless driving was to lose his driver's license.

6. **grievance:** (n.) problem causing resentment or complaint; grounds for resentment or complaint.
   Example: The complaining students took their *grievance* to the principal.

7. **pernicious:** (adj.) harmful, destructive, lethal.
   Example: The *pernicious* fumes of ammonia gas spread over the city.

scene iii

8. **warrant:** (v.) to give adequate reasons for; to state with conviction.

   Example: The used car salesperson *warranted* that the car had been driven only on weekends.

scene v

9. **purge:** (v.) cleanse, forgive, absolve.

   Example: With vigorous scrubbing, Dad *purged* the stain from the carpet.

10. **solemnity:** (n.) being formal, dignified.

    Example: In contrast to the *solemnity* of the wedding, the bride skipped down the aisle.

NAME:_____   DATE:_____

Prereading Activity
for
Romeo and Juliet
Plot Summaries
Act I

Directions: To help you better understand and follow Shakespeare's play, read the summary of specific scenes immediately before you begin to read the original. If you get lost during the scene, refer to the summary again.

Prologue   In these sixteen lines, the Chorus establishes the setting as Verona, an Italian city. Its warring, noble families are again fighting over an old dispute. The children of both families become lovers and their deaths ultimately end the feud.

Act I, scene i   On a Saturday afternoon, Sampson and Gregory, servants of the Capulets, joke with each other and brag about what each would do if he encountered members of the Montague household, their sworn enemies. Seeing Abraham and Balthasar, servants of the Montagues, Sampson insults them by biting his thumb. This starts a fight. Benvolio, Romeo's cousin, stops the fight only to be drawn into it again by Tybalt, Lady Capulet's hot-tempered nephew.

Escalus, the Prince, breaks up the fight and declares if another fight occurs both Capulet and Montague will be put to death. Capulet leaves with the Prince while Lord and Lady Montague remain behind.

The Montagues then ask Benvolio to explain the cause of the fight, which he does. Then they ask about their son Romeo. Benvolio has seen Romeo wandering about the edge of the city, acting strangely. Later Romeo admits to Benvolio that Romeo has fallen in love with Rosaline, but is out of favor with her.

Act I, scene ii   Paris, a kinsman of the Prince, asks Lord Capulet for permission to marry his daughter Juliet. Although Capulet feels she is too young, his only concern is that his last remaining child be happy. He consents to marriage only if Juliet is in love. Capulet gives an illiterate servant a list of people to invite to a party that night. The servant seeks help of strangers in the street, Romeo and Benvolio. When the young men discover that Rosaline is on the list, they decide to crash the party.

Act I, scene iii   Lady Capulet, while being interrupted frequently by the Nurse, manages to ask Juliet how she feels about being married. Juliet makes no promise to consent unless she likes what she sees when she meets Paris that evening.

Act I, scene iv

Later that evening in the street, Romeo and his friends, Benvolio and Mercutio, a cousin of the Prince, have put on masks to crash the party at the Capulets'. Mercutio delivers the "Queen Mab" speech. Queen Mab is the fairy queen that Mercutio describes as coming to bewitch men in her tiny carriage made of a hazelnut shell, with a cover of grasshoppers' wings and wagon spokes of spiders' legs, all drawn by motes driven by a liveried gnat. Before leaving for the party, Romeo states that he fears some serious events will result from this evening.

Act I, scene v

At the Capulets', Lord Capulet makes his guests welcome. When Romeo (who had come to see Rosaline) sees Juliet, he falls in love with her immediately. Not knowing that she is his family's enemy, he woos Juliet by comparing her to a holy shrine and his lips to religious pilgrims that journey to it. With their kiss, they realize they are in love.

Meanwhile, Tybalt recognizes Romeo and informs Lord Capulet that their enemy mocks them by crashing the party. Capulet decides not to make an issue and lets Romeo and his friends stay.

Romeo discovers Juliet's identity and leaves. Juliet sends the Nurse to discover her new lover's identity. When Juliet learns that Romeo is her enemy, she also recognizes that it is too late, for now, she too, is in love.

Class Period:

CHARACTER ASSIGNMENTS FOR ORAL READING GROUPS
Romeo and Juliet

Session 1: Prologue, Act I, scenes i and ii

Characters	*Group 1*	*Group 2*	*Group 3*	*Group 4*
Chorus, Abraham, Lord Capulet	_____	_____	_____	_____
Sampson, Officer, Paris	_____	_____	_____	_____
Gregory, Citizens, Servant (Clown)	_____	_____	_____	_____
Benvolio	_____	_____	_____	_____
Lord Montague	_____	_____	_____	_____
Lady Montague	_____	_____	_____	_____
Prince	_____	_____	_____	_____

33

Class Period:

CHARACTER ASSIGNMENTS FOR ORAL READING GROUPS

Romeo and Juliet

Session 2: Act I, scenes iii, iv, v

Characters	*Group 1*	*Group 2*	*Group 3*	*Group 4*
Juliet, First Servant	_____	_____	_____	_____
Lady Capulet, Second Servant	_____	_____	_____	_____
Nurse, Third Servant	_____	_____	_____	_____
Romeo, Old Capulet	_____	_____	_____	_____
Benvolio, Fourth Servant	_____	_____	_____	_____
Mercutio	_____	_____	_____	_____
Lord Capulet	_____	_____	_____	_____
Tybalt	_____	_____	_____	_____

34

NAME:_____ DATE: _____

During-Reading Activity
for
Romeo and Juliet
Directions for Response Journal

Although we often read silently, reading is an active process. As we run our eyes across a line of text, we transform the letters and words into mental images. The words have the power to affect us in many ways. This response journal will help you state several different types of responses immediately after you've read and assist you in recalling the experiences of reading before discussing them with your classmates.

Your response journal is a place for you to react to what you read personally. This is a place to begin piecing together your understanding of the play. Your journal is a place to think aloud on paper and not have to worry about grammatical correctness or punctuation. You may wish to do it as you read or immediately upon finishing a reading session. It won't be nearly as effective if you put it off! There are four types of responses you should make each time. None of these needs to be more than a brief paragraph. You will have a total of four paragraphs.

1. *Respond emotionally.* How does the play make you feel at this point? Record your emotions in a few sentences and then try to figure out why you feel as you do.

2. *Make associations between ideas in the text and your personal experience.* In what situations have you felt similarly to the characters? What persons, places, ideas from your own experiences came to your mind while you were reading this portion of the play? List three to five associations, but don't worry about why they came to mind. Just accept that they occur.

3. *Look at the language.* What portions of Shakespeare's language attracts your attention? These might be individual words, phrases, lines, scenes, or images. Make note of whatever feature(s) draw your attention. Speculate for a few minutes about what you think these might mean.

4. *Record any questions or problems.* Make note of any portion of the play, its language, or events that seem to cause you problems. Write down any questions that occur to you as you read.

35

Here's a sample journal for the Act I, scene iii:

1. The Nurse certainly does like to hear herself talk! Small wonder Lady Capulet becomes impatient. Juliet doesn't seem to know very much about love and marriage. I like the honesty of her wait-and-see attitude.

2. I get impatient when my sister monopolizes the conversation.
I've taken a wait-and-see attitude when presented with meeting new people.
When the Nurse talks about her daughter playing with Juliet, I remember watching the children in my neighborhood play together.

3. Juliet's line: "I'll look to like, if looking liking move."
I like the way the meaning shifts with each form of *look* and *like*.

4. What does the Nurse mean when she says "women grow by men"?

NAME:_____   DATE:_____

During-Reading Activity
for
Romeo and Juliet
Response Journal

Directions: Use the spaces below to record your responses to the acts and scenes of *Romeo and Juliet* that you've just finished reading. Respond in all four ways and take a few additional minutes to explore why you responded as you did.

Response Journal for Act ____, scene ____ to Act ____, scene ____.

1.   How does the play make you feel at this point? Record your emotional response(s) in a few sentences and then explore them for a few minutes, trying to figure out why you feel as you do.

2.   In what situations have you felt similarly to the characters? What persons, places, ideas from your own experiences came to your mind while you were reading this portion of the play? Try to list at least three associations, but don't worry about why they came to mind. Just accept that they occur.

   a.

   b.

   c.

3. What portions of Shakespeare's language attracts your attention? These might be individual words, phrases, lines, scenes, or images. Make note of whatever features draw your attention. Speculate for a few minutes about what you think these might mean.

4. Make note of any portion of the play, its language, or events that seem to cause you problems. Note any questions that you might ask.

NAME:_____   DATE:_____

During-Reading Activity
for
Romeo and Juliet
Directions for Character Diary

As you read *Romeo and Juliet*, you will find that the events of the play affect the lives of some twenty characters, not just the lives of Romeo and Juliet. To give you an opportunity to explore the reactions of other characters, pretend to be one of the lesser characters. For this assignment, you will keep the personal diary of a single character for the one week during which the play takes place.

Select one of the following characters for your diary:

Escalus, Prince of Verona	Lord Montague
Lord Capulet	Benvolio
Friar Laurence	Balthasar
Peter, the Nurse's servant	Lady Capulet
Juliet's Nurse	

In your diary, record the events of the day and provide an explanation for how your character may have heard of them, if the character was not involved with the events directly. For example, Escalus, the Prince, only speaks in Acts I, III, and V; however, his guards or advisors would keep him well informed of the events in the city. His diary for Wednesday might look like this:

Wednesday, July 22, 1597

Today should have been a happy one for us. Our kinsman, Paris, was to have married Capulet's fair daughter, Juliet. Capulet, a rich but often vulgar man, had spent much in preparation for the banquet to celebrate the day. His troubles seemed to be coming to an end. Our men tell me that Juliet had at first refused to obey her father and be married until she sought counsel from a Franciscan friar and then agreed to the marriage. The family seemed happy in spite of their grief over the death of Tybalt, Lady Capulet's nephew.

That same brawl on Sunday brought the death of our kinsman, Mercutio. We are saddened by his death, for we shall sorely miss the quickness of his wit.

We wonder why a child like Juliet would take her own life when she had so much happiness ahead?

My man tells me that young Romeo, son of Montague, has obeyed our decree and is banished to Mantua, a day's ride across the mountains.

Keep in mind that your character will write about events after they've happened. For example, your diary entry that records the events of Sunday morning wouldn't be written until Sunday afternoon. Use the following sequence to help you understand events according to acts:

Act	*Time Covered in Character Diary*
I	Saturday
II	Early Sunday morning through Sunday afternoon
III	Sunday afternoon through Monday just after dawn
IV	Monday through Wednesday dawn
V	Thursday until just before dawn Friday

NAME:_____ DATE:_____

During-Reading Activity
for
Romeo and Juliet
Character Diary 1
Act I
Saturday

Directions: Use the space below to record your character's reactions to the events that occur in Act I of *Romeo and Juliet*. Remember to include a summary of events, explain how your character learned of them, and give your character's reactions to them. Because the act contains five scenes, you may wish to record your character's entries as you read each scene. If you need additional room, use the back of this sheet.

The Personal Diary of

_____
(character's name)

Saturday, July 19, 1597

_____
_____
_____
_____
_____
_____
_____
_____
_____
_____
_____
_____
_____
_____
_____
_____
_____

NAME:_____   DATE:_____

During-Reading Activity
for
Romeo and Juliet
Viewing Act I, scene v
Romeo and Juliet's First Meeting

Directions: After you've read this scene, viewing a film or video version may help you better understand how the text translates into characters' actions. Although you may want to keep your copy of the play handy, don't be surprised if the actors' script varies from yours. Film scripts often delete or reorder the lines in the play. You may want to note questions you need to ask your teacher afterwards. After viewing the scene, take a few minutes to respond to the questions below.

1. What do the costumes, the set representing the Capulets' house, and the stage properties (like the food, trays, goblets, and tableware) tell you about Lord Capulet's position in the community?

2. What seems to be Romeo's immediate reaction when he first sees Juliet across the room? What seems to be Juliet's? How do the actors' facial expressions, tones of voice, and gestures enhance Shakespeare's words?

3. How does Tybalt react to Romeo's crashing the party? How do both Lord and Lady Capulet respond to Tybalt?

© 1993 by The Center for Applied Research in Education

NAME:_____   DATE:_____

During-Reading Activity
for
Romeo and Juliet
Guide to Character Development: Romeo
Act I

Shakespeare reveals his characters in four ways:

* through what the characters say to other characters in dialogue;

* through what the characters reveal about their thoughts through long speeches to the audience called *soliloquies*;

* through what other characters say about them;

* through what they do, their actions.

As you read the play, examine the following scenes for what they reveal about Romeo's character and fill in the chart briefly using your own words. If you need more room, use the back of the page.

Scene	What Romeo says, does, or what others say about him	What this reveals about Romeo's character
Act I, scene i After the street fight		
Act I, scene ii When Romeo helps Capulet's illiterate servant		
Act I, scene iv Before Romeo and the others crash the banquet		
Act I, scene v Romeo meets Juliet		

During-Reading Activity
for
Romeo and Juliet
Guide to Character Development: Juliet
Act I

Shakespeare reveals his characters in four ways:

- through what the characters say to other characters in dialogue;
- through what the characters reveal about their thoughts through long speeches to the audience called *soliloquies*;
- through what other characters say about them;
- through what they do, their actions.

As you read the play, examine the following scenes for what they reveal about Juliet's character and fill in the chart briefly using your own words. If you need more room, use the back of the page.

Scene	What Juliet says, does, or what others say about her	What this reveals about Juliet's character
Act I, scene iii When Lady Capulet asks Juliet about marriage		
Act I, scene v Juliet meets Romeo for the first time		

NAME:_____ DATE:_____

During-Reading Activity
for
Romeo and Juliet
Guide to Character Development: Mercutio
Act I

Shakespeare reveals his characters in four ways:

- through what the characters say to other characters in dialogue;
- through what the characters reveal about their thoughts through long speeches to the audience called *soliloquies*;
- through what other characters say about them;
- through what they do, their actions.

As you read the play, examine the following scenes for what they reveal about Mercutio's character and fill in the chart briefly using your own words. If you need more room, use the back of the page.

Scene	What Mercutio says, does, or what others say about him	What this reveals about Mercutio's character
Act I, scene iv Before he crashes the Capulets' banquet		

During-Reading Activity
for
Romeo and Juliet
Guide to Character Development: Nurse
Act I

Shakespeare reveals his characters in four ways:

- ❧ through what the characters say to other characters in dialogue;
- ❧ through what the characters reveal about their thoughts through long speeches to the audience called *soliloquies*;
- ❧ through what other characters say about them;
- ❧ through what they do, their actions.

As you read the play, examine the following scenes for what they reveal about the Nurse's character and fill in the chart briefly using your own words. If you need more room, use the back of the page.

Scene	What the Nurse says, does, or what others say about her	What this reveals about the Nurse's character
Act I, scene iii Lady Capulet asks Juliet about marriage		
Act I, scene v Juliet meets Romeo		

NAME:_____   DATE:_____

Postreading Activity
for
Romeo and Juliet
Comprehension Check
Act I

Directions: After you've read all of the Prologue and Act I, use the following questions to check how well you've understood what you've read. For each question, select the most appropriate answer from the choices listed below it. Place the letter corresponding to your answer in the space to the left of the item number.

_____1.   At the end of the street fight in scene i, what does Escalus, the Prince of Verona, threaten to do if the Capulet and Montague families get into another fight?

A. Kill the person who starts the next fight.
B. Banish both Lord Capulet and Lord Montague.
C. Kill both Capulet and Montague.
D. Banish the person who starts the fight.
E. Behead both Lord Capulet and Lord Montague.

_____2.   How do Romeo and his friends learn that Rosaline will be invited to the Capulets' party?

A. Rosaline sends Romeo a note.
B. They see a copy of the guest list.
C. Juliet tells them.
D. The Nurse tells them accidentally.
E. Mercutio has been invited.

_____3.   In scene ii, Paris asks Lord Capulet for permission to marry Juliet. What condition does Capulet add with these lines?

ફ

My will to her consent is but a part.
And she agree, within her scope of choice
Lies my consent and fair according voice.

ફ

A. He will give his permission tomorrow.
B. Paris must ask Juliet himself.
C. Lord Capulet will order Juliet to marry Paris.

47

      D. Lord Capulet will agree if Juliet agrees.

      E. Lord Capulet refuses but Juliet may accept for herself.

_____ 4. After the Nurse tells Romeo that Juliet is a Capulet, he replies

ک

Is she a Capulet?
O dear account! my life is my foe's debt.

ک

What do these lines suggest about how Romeo feels about having fallen in love with Juliet?

A. Romeo has sworn his love and life to his enemy.
B. Romeo owes Juliet an explanation.
C. Juliet owes Romeo her life.
D. Romeo must escape before he is caught.
E. Juliet owes him an explanation.

_____ 5. In scene iv, Benvolio urges Romeo and his friends to enter the Capulets' party before the food is gone. Romeo replies that he fears their mischief will lead so some unfortunate end. Now that Romeo and Juliet have fallen in love with each other, in what ways are Romeo's fears justified?

A. Both Romeo and Juliet have fallen in love with their sworn enemies.
B. Both recognize and accept the danger of loving their enemy.
C. Tybalt has recognized Romeo at the party and vowed revenge.
D. A, B, and C.
E. A and B.
F. B and C.
G. All of these.

© 1993 by The Center for Applied Research in Education

NAME:_____   DATE:_____

Postreading Activity
for
Romeo and Juliet
Small Group Discussion to Check Comprehension
Act I

Directions: After you've read all of the Prologue and Act I, discuss each of the following questions in small groups briefly. Use the space below each question to note points you may wish to share later. If you need more room, use the back of the page.

1. At the end of the street fight in scene 1, what does Escalus, the Prince of Verona, threaten to do if the Capulet and Montague families get into another fight?

2. How do Romeo and his friends learn that Rosaline will be invited to Capulet's party?

3. In scene ii, Paris asks Lord Capulet for permission to marry Juliet. What condition does Capulet add with these lines?:

    ❧

    My will to her consent is but a part.
    And she agree, within her scope of choice
    Lies my consent and fair according voice.

    ❧

4. After the Nurse tells Romeo that Juliet is a Capulet, he replies

    ❧

    Is she a Capulet?
    O dear account! my life is my foe's debt.

    ❧

    What do these lines suggest about how Romeo feels about having fallen in love with Juliet?

5. In scene iv, Benvolio urges Romeo and his friends to enter the Capulets' party before the food is gone. Romeo replies that he fears their mischief will lead to some unfortunate end. Now that Romeo and Juliet have fallen in love with each other, in what ways are Romeo's fears justified or unjustified?

NAME:_____   DATE:_____

Postreading Activity
for
Romeo and Juliet
Critical Thinking Questions
Act I

Directions: To help develop your understanding of Act I, take time to think about and discuss these questions. The first question is the focus question and the point of the discussion. Don't be concerned that you may not be able to answer it at first. Proceed to the exploration questions and then return to the focus question.

Focus Question. If you were either Romeo or Juliet, how do you think your parents would react to your telling them the news that you had fallen in love suddenly with the child of their sworn enemy?

Exploration Questions.

1. Think back to a situation where someone made a strong first impression on you. What was your reaction? What factors contributed to it?

2. What other characters in the literature that you've studied have had an instant reaction (either good or bad) to each other? What was the reaction and how did the characters account for it?

3. How do Romeo and Juliet react to each other when they first meet?

4. If you were Romeo or Juliet, how would you know that you were in love instantly? How do they know?

5. How does society feel about the idea of people falling in love instantly? Why do you think people feel this way?

6. When you react with strong emotions to a situation, how do others around respond to you?

Postreading Activity
for
Romeo and Juliet
Language Exploration:
Changed Word Order
Act I

To obtain the meter of the lines, Shakespeare often changes the normal order of words, placing words so that the naturally stressed syllables fall into the rhythmic pattern. Although Shakespeare's language was probably understood more easily in Elizabethan England, his verse sentences do not always proceed as directly as today's normally spoken or written English. In our daily spoken English, we change word order to ask questions but not generally to make statements.

To understand some lines of the play, try turning the sentence around. For example, Benvolio begins his explanation of the fight to Lord Montague by saying,

ꝛ

Here were the servants of your adversary,
And yours, close fighting ere I did approach.

(Act I, scene i)

ꝛ

In more traditional sentence order he might say,

ꝛ

Your adversary's servants and yours were here,
closely fighting, as I did approach.

ꝛ

Here are other sentences from the text and their reordering:

Original	*Reordered*
Well in that hit you miss.	*You miss* well in that hit.
Do I live dead that live to tell thee so.	*I do live* dead that live to tell thee so.
Take thou some new infection to thy eye.	*Thou take* some new infection to your eye.

Directions: Working in pairs, small groups, or as your teacher directs, try reordering these lines. Once you've written your results, go back to the scene and look at the lines in context.

1. And too soon marred are those so early made (Capulet, scene ii).

2. At this ancient feast of Capulet's
   Sups the fair Rosaline. . . .(Benvolio, scene ii).

3. Come Lammas Eve at night shall she be fourteen (Nurse, scene iii).

4. And sometime comes she with a tithe-pig's tail (Mercutio, scene iv).

5. And then dreams he of cutting foreign throats (Mercutio, scene iv).

6. Then dreams he of smelling out a suit (Mercutio, scene iv).

7. She I swear hath corns (Capulet, scene v).

8. So shows a snowy dove trooping with crows
   As yonder lady o'er her fellow shows. (Romeo, scene v).

9. Then have my lips the sin that they have took (Juliet, scene v).

10. To strike him dead, I hold it not a sin. (Tybalt, scene v).

© 1993 by The Center for Applied Research in Education

Postreading Activity
for
Romeo and Juliet
Vocabulary in Context
Act I

Directions: In each of the passages below you will find one of the words from the prereading vocabulary list for Act I. Review the definitions given in the prereading vocabulary. Working individually, in pairs, or in small groups as your teacher directs, examine each of the underlined words in the following passages from Act I. For each word, use the appropriate meaning and develop a brief interpretation of the passage within the context of the play.

1. Lord Montague (Act I, i), speaking of Romeo's lovesickness:

Many a morning hath he there been seen,
With tears <u>augmenting</u> the fresh morning dew,

2. Benvolio (Act I, i), explaining how the street fight started to Lord Montague and the Prince:

Here were the servants of your <u>adversary</u>,
And yours, close fighting ere I did approach.

3. Benvolio (Act I, i), asking Romeo about Rosaline:

Then she hath sworn that she will still live <u>chaste</u>?

© 1993 by The Center for Applied Research in Education

4.   Romeo (Act I, i), describing Rosaline's eyes to Benvolio:

&

'Tis the way
To call hers, <u>exquisite</u>, in question more.

&

5.   Prince (Act I, i), declaring his penalty upon Lords Capulet and Montague if there is more street fighting:

&

Your lives shall pay the <u>forfeit</u> of the peace.

&

6.   Benvolio (Act I, i), telling Lord Montague that he will ask Romeo why he seems so sad:

&

See where he comes, so please you step aside.
I'll know his <u>grievance</u> or be much denied.

&

7.   The Prince (Act I, i), scolding the men for fighting in the streets:

&

What ho, you men, you beasts,
That quench the fire of your <u>pernicious</u> rage.

&

8. Nurse (Act I, iii), telling Lady Capulet a story about Juliet as a child:

    ❧

    I <u>warrant</u>, an I should live a thousand years,
    I never should forget it.

    ❧

9. Romeo (Act I, v), speaking to Juliet at the banquet:

    ❧

    Thus from my lips, by thine, my sin is <u>purged</u>.

    ❧

10. Tybalt (Act I, v), commenting on Romeo crashing the banquet:

    ❧

    What dares the slave
    Come hither covered with an antic face
    To fleer and scorn at our <u>solemnity</u>?

    ❧

NAME:_____   DATE:_____

Vocabulary Review Quiz
for
Romeo and Juliet
Act I

Directions: For each of the italicized words in the sentences below, determine which letter best reflects the use of the word in this context. Place the letter corresponding to your answer in the space to the left of the item number.

_____ 1. The Prince threatened Lords Capulet and Montague that their lives would be the *forfeit* if another feud occurred between their families.
In this context, *forfeit* means

A. loss   B. unit of measurement   C. penalty   D. prediction

_____ 2. The Nurse is eager to *warrant* the truth of nearly every story she tells.
In this context, *warrant* means

A. arrest   B. complain a lot about   C. lie about
D. state with conviction

_____ 3. Although Rosaline is *chaste*, she still flirts with Romeo.
In this context, *chaste* means

A. followed closely   B. believable and reasonable
C. modest and decent   D. immoral

_____ 4. Romeo feels that Rosaline's eyes are *exquisite*.
In this context, *exquisite* means

A. especially beautiful   B. almond-shaped   C. small   D. precise

_____ 5. Tybalt, Lady Capulet's nephew, sees himself as Romeo's chief *adversary*.
In this context, *adversary* means

A. celebration   B. foe   C. friend   D. relative

_____ 6. Not knowing the exact cause of the feud between the Capulets and Montagues *augments* the pettiness of the revenge.
In this context, *augments* means

A. transports   B. increases   C. lessens   D. releases

_____ 7. When Romeo and his friends crash the Capulets' party, Tybalt feels he has a *grievance* against them.
In this context, *grievance* means

A. sadness   B. sorrow   C. complaint   D. determination

_____ 8. Romeo told Juliet that her kiss would *purge* any sin from his lips.
In this context, *purge* means

A. absolve   B. resolve   C. dissolve   D. harm

_____ 9. The Prince sees the hatred between the Capulets and Montagues as
pernicious.
In this context, *pernicious* means

A. petty   B. silly   C. curious   D. destructive

_____ 10. Tybalt feels that the banquet is an occasion for great *solemnity*.
In this context, *solemnity* means

A. lonely   B. anger   C. dignity   D. foolishness

PROLOGUE
AND
ACT II

© 1993 by The Center for Applied Research in Education

NAME:_____   **DATE:**_____

Focusing Activities
for
Romeo and Juliet
Scenarios for Improvisation
Prologue and Act II

Directions: Provided below are locations and situations involving characters. Before reading an individual scene, pretend to be one of the characters and act out the situation. Don't worry about speaking like characters in Shakespeare's play; just try to imagine how you would react to the situation and use your own language. Take a few minutes to discuss with the other performers what you would like to do. Be prepared to act out your scene for others in the class. Afterward, classmates outside your group may discuss what they've seen.

scene i.   *Scene:* Friar Laurence's cell at the local monastery the morning after the party at the Capulets'.

Characters: Romeo and Friar Laurence, a priest.

Situation: Romeo tells the priest that he has fallen in love again. This time, however, is different because it's with Juliet, the daughter of his enemy. The priest, who has often advised Romeo when he has fallen in love, offers advice. Improvise the dialogue between them.

scene iv.   *Scene:* A street in the middle of Verona, Sunday morning.

Characters: Romeo and Juliet's Nurse.

Situation: The Nurse has been sent by Juliet to find out what Romeo's plans are. What does Romeo tell her? How does the Nurse, who wants Juliet to be happy, respond?

Focusing Activities
for
Romeo and Juliet
Small Group Discussion Questions
Prologue and Act II

Directions: Before reading scenes in Act II, discuss the questions in small groups. You may want to make notes about your discussion, so you can share them with classmates or refer back to them after you've read the scene.

Prologue. Now that Romeo and Juliet have met and fallen in love, knowing who each other is, what do you think they will do?

scene i. How do you think Romeo's cousin, Benvolio, or friend, Mercutio, would react if Romeo told him about being in love with Juliet, daughter of his family's enemy?

scene ii.

1. Now that Romeo has slipped away from his friends, where do you think he will go and what will he do there?

2. Now that the party is over, what do you think Juliet will do knowing who Romeo is?

scene iii. What plans does Romeo need to make before he meets Juliet's messenger? If you were Romeo, to whom would you go for assistance?

scene iv. In Act II, scene ii, Juliet promised to send a messenger to Romeo to learn of his plans. Whom do you think she might send and why?

scene v. If you were Juliet, what emotions might you feel while waiting for the Nurse to return with news of Romeo's plans?

scene vi. What issues or problems might Friar Laurence recognize in planning to marry Romeo and Juliet that the lovers might not?

© 1993 by The Center for Applied Research in Education

Focusing Activities
for
Romeo and Juliet
Speculation Journal
Prologue and Act II

Directions: This activity will allow you to become involved actively with reading the play by helping you to determine a definite purpose for reading. Before you read these scenes in Act II, take a few minutes to respond in writing to the questions below. Don't worry about correct answers here. Use your own experience or what you have read in the play to speculate about what you think will happen. After reading a scene you may find that characters reacted differently than you thought. Don't worry about these differences; just make note of them because you will have opportunities to share these differences in other activities.

Prologue and scene i. Based upon what you know about Romeo's friends, Benvolio and Mercutio, how do you think they will react to the news of Romeo's falling in love with Juliet?

scene ii. Speculate about one of these two questions:

1. As Romeo, a 17-year-old boy, you have just seen and fallen in love with Juliet. Describe the situation and your feelings as you might in a personal diary or journal.

2. As Juliet, a girl two weeks from her fourteenth birthday, you have just seen and fallen in love with Romeo. Describe the situation and your feelings as you might in a personal diary or journal.

scene iii.   Friar Laurence is a Franciscan monk and Romeo's friend. How do you think he will react to Romeo's falling in and out of love so easily?

scene iv.   How do you think Mercutio will respond to Tybalt's threat of revenge upon Romeo and his friends?

scene v.   If you were Juliet, what thoughts would go through your mind while you waited for the Nurse to return from meeting Romeo?

scene vi.   If you were Friar Laurence, what problems do you foresee for Romeo and Juliet if they marry?

After Reading Act II: Now that you have finished reading the act, which of your speculations were most accurate? How do you account for them? Which ones were least like the action of the play? Why do you think you speculated as you did?

NAME:_____   DATE:_____

Prereading Activity
for
Romeo and Juliet
Vocabulary
Prologue and Act II

Directions: Shakespeare uses the following words in Act II. The section below provides a brief definition of each word and provides a sentence to illustrate its meaning.

Definitions.

scene ii

1. **conjure:** (v.) to charge, entreat, charm, bewitch; to call upon or command a spirit using a spell.

   Example: Broomhilda the witch tried to *conjure* a spirit but failed.

2. **envious:** (v.) full of jealousy for another's possessions.

   Example: Because Billy was *envious* of Sally's new toy, he snatched it away from her.

3. **peril:** (n.) exposure to injury, risk, danger.

   Example: Each week, cartoon super heroes must survive some new *peril*.

4. **perverse:** (adj.) determined not to do what is expected, contrary.

   Example: Robin Williams is known for his *perverse* sense of humor.

5. **procure:** (v.) to obtain or get through effort.

   Example: By rummaging around in Grandma's attic, we *procured* wonderful Halloween costumes from old clothes.

scene iii

6. **chide:** (v.) to scold; to find fault.

   Example: Mrs. Smith *chided* her son into apologizing for being mean to his little sister.

7. **distemper:** (v.) to put out of temper, to disturb, to sicken.

   Example: A severe case of the flu *distempered* Grace's usually pleasant personality.

65

8. **inter-cession:** (n.) the act of pleading or asking something for another person.

Example: When Jim wrecked Dad's car, my *intercession* was to break the news to Dad.

9. **perjury:** (n.) the act of swearing falsely, a lie.

Example: Ben Matlock showed that the real murderer had committed *perjury* when she lied while testifying.

scene v

10. **herald:** (n.) messenger. (v.) to announce.

Example: The blooming tulips *herald* the return of spring.

Prereading Activity
for
Romeo and Juliet
Plot Summaries
Prologue and Act II

Directions: To help you better understand and follow Shakespeare's play, read the summary of specific scenes immediately before you begin to read the original. If you get lost during the scene, refer to the summary again.

Prologue The Chorus both comments upon Romeo and Juliet having fallen in love with their sworn enemies (lines 1–5) and speculates upon the outcome of their love (lines 6–15). Both Romeo and Juliet, as young people who have often desired love, have unknowingly found it in their sworn enemies. They find it is not quite as charming as they thought it would be. Filled with passion, however, they are willing to meet secretly.

Act II, Late Saturday night or early Sunday morning, Romeo sneaks down
scene i the road outside Capulet's orchard. Questioning whether he can go back now, he climbs the wall. Benvolio, Mercutio, and others come down the lane looking for Romeo, calling his name. Mercutio pretends that Romeo is dead of love for Rosaline and tries to raise Romeo's ghost again by calling upon the magic of Rosaline's spirit.

Act II, Romeo remains in the shadows as he sees Juliet on her balcony. Struck
scene ii by her beauty, he compares Juliet to the sun, outshining the moon. When she leans her head on her hand, Romeo wishes to be a glove on it, in order to touch her cheek.

Juliet continues speaking aloud, unaware of Romeo. She wishes Romeo weren't a Montague, but concludes that his name, not his person, is the enemy. When Romeo speaks, startling Juliet, he tells her that he would change his name for her happiness.

Juliet is afraid for Romeo's safety; if he's caught, the Capulets will kill him. Caught up in love, Romeo fears nothing. They swear their love to each other. Juliet tells Romeo if he is honorable, then he will marry her. She agrees to send a messenger the next day to find out the details. After many delays, they part.

*Act II,
scene iii*

Shortly after dawn on Sunday, Friar Laurence gathers herbs and wild-flowers to make medicines. When Romeo appears, the friar notices that Romeo has been out all night. The friar asks if he's been with Rosaline. Romeo tells the priest that he is now in love with Juliet. Friar Laurence scolds Romeo for falling in and out of love too quickly. Although Romeo tries to convince the monk that he is truly in love, Friar Laurence advises him to proceed slowly with love.

*Act II,
scene iv*

While Romeo has been conferring with the friar, Benvolio and Mercutio continue to search the streets for Romeo. Tybalt, Lady Capulet's nephew, has sent a letter challenging Romeo to a duel for crashing the party. Mercutio and Benvolio point out Tybalt's skill as a swordsman.

When Romeo appears, Mercutio accuses him of having spent the night with a French prostitute and is irritated that Romeo gave them the slip. Mercutio teases Romeo, who takes it in good humor.

The Nurse, who, acting as Juliet's messenger has dressed in her best clothes and tries to act like a lady, comes to meet Romeo in the square. Mercutio and Benvolio, thinking she is a prostitute, taunt her when she asks for Romeo. Romeo finally sends his friends home and speaks to the Nurse. Romeo tells the Nurse that Juliet should come to Friar Laurence's cell, where they will be married that afternoon. Romeo also tells the Nurse to meet Balthasar, his servant, to get a rope ladder, so Romeo can sneak into the house later that night.

*Act II,
scene v*

Juliet paces the orchard waiting for the Nurse to return. The nurse was to have been back at 9:30, but it is now shortly after noon. When the Nurse does return, she is tired and wishes to rest before delivering Romeo's message. Only when the Nurse is certain that she and Juliet are alone does she deliver the message. The Nurse hurries Juliet to the meeting while she goes to collect the ladder.

*Act II,
Scene vi*

Friar Laurence warns Romeo that the young man may be caught up in his passion and warns him to proceed cautiously. When Romeo and Juliet meet, Friar Laurence is convinced that they are truly in love. Hoping to end the feud, Friar Laurence agrees to marry them.

© 1993 by The Center for Applied Research in Education

Class Period:

CHARACTER ASSIGNMENTS FOR ORAL READING GROUPS
Romeo and Juliet

Session 3: Prologue, Act II, scenes i, ii, iii

Characters	_Group 1_	_Group 2_	_Group 3_	_Group 4_
Chorus	_____	_____	_____	_____
Romeo (scenes i and ii)	_____	_____	_____	_____
Romeo (scene iii)	_____	_____	_____	_____
Benvolio	_____	_____	_____	_____
Mercutio	_____	_____	_____	_____
Juliet	_____	_____	_____	_____
Nurse	_____	_____	_____	_____
Friar Laurence	_____	_____	_____	_____

Class Period:

CHARACTER ASSIGNMENTS FOR ORAL READING GROUPS

Romeo and Juliet

Session 4: Act II, scenes iv, v, vi

Characters	*Group 1*	*Group 2*	*Group 3*	*Group 4*
Mercutio				
Benvolio				
Romeo				
Nurse (scene iv)				
Nurse (scene vi)				
Peter				
Juliet				
Friar Laurence				

70

NAME:_____   DATE:_____

During-Reading Activity
for
Romeo and Juliet
Character Diary 2
Act II
Sunday Morning and Early Afternoon

Directions: Use the space below to record your character's reactions to the events that occur in Act II of *Romeo and Juliet*. Remember to include a summary of events, explain how your character learned of them, and give your character's reactions to these events.

The Personal Diary of

_____
(character's name)

Sunday, July 20, 1597
Afternoon

_____
_____
_____
_____
_____
_____
_____
_____
_____
_____
_____
_____
_____
_____
_____

During-Reading Activity
for
Romeo and Juliet
Viewing Act II, scene ii
The First Balcony Scene

Directions: After you've read this scene, viewing a film or video version may help you better understand how the text translates into characters' actions. Although you may want to keep your copy of the play handy, don't be surprised if the actors' script varies from yours. Film scripts often delete or reorder the lines in the play. You may want to note questions you want to ask your teacher afterwards. After viewing the scene, take a few minutes to respond to the questions below.

1. What obstacles has Romeo had to overcome to get into Capulet's orchard?

2. What seems to be Romeo's immediate reaction when he first sees Juliet on her balcony? What seems to be Juliet's reaction when she first realizes Romeo is there? How do the actors' facial expressions, tones of voice, and gestures enhance Shakespeare's words?

3. What kinds of things does the director of the film or video version do to depict this scene that a director could not do in a production of a stage play?

During-Reading Activity
for
Romeo and Juliet
Guide to Character Development: Romeo
Act II

Shakespeare reveals his characters in four ways:

- through what the characters say to other characters in dialogue;
- through what the characters reveal about their thoughts through long speeches to the audience called *soliloquies*;
- through what other characters say about them;
- through what they do, their actions.

As you read the play, examine the following scenes for what they reveal about Romeo's character and fill in the chart briefly using your own words. If you need more room, use the back of the page.

Scene	What Romeo says, does, or what others say about him	What this reveals about Romeo's character
Act II, scenes i and ii Romeo slips away from his friends and meets Juliet		
Act II, scene iii Romeo meets with Friar Laurence		
Act II, scene iv Romeo meets Mercutio in the street; Romeo meets with the Nurse		
Act II, scene vi Romeo marries Juliet		

NAME:_____   DATE:_____

During-Reading Activity
for
Romeo and Juliet
Guide to Character Development: Juliet
Act II

Shakespeare reveals his characters in four ways:

- ❧ through what the characters say to other characters in dialogue;
- ❧ through what the characters reveal about their thoughts through long speeches to the audience called *soliloquies*;
- ❧ through what other characters say about them;
- ❧ through what they do, their actions.

As you read the play, examine the following scenes for what they reveal about Juliet's character and fill in the chart briefly using your own words. If you need more room, use the back of the page.

Scene	What Juliet says, does, or what others say about her	What this reveals about Juliet's character
Act II, scene ii Juliet meets Romeo on her balcony		
Act II, scene v Juliet learns of Romeo's plans from the Nurse		
Act II, scene vi Juliet marries Romeo		

© 1993 by The Center for Applied Research in Education

NAME:_____   DATE:_____

During-Reading Activity
for
Romeo and Juliet
Guide to Character Development: Mercutio
Act II

Shakespeare reveals his characters in four ways:

ও through what the characters say to other characters in dialogue;

ও through what the characters reveal about their thoughts through long speeches to the audience called *soliloquies*;

ও through what other characters say about them;

ও through what they do, their actions.

As you read the play, examine the following scenes for what they reveal about Mercutio's character and fill in the chart briefly using your own words. If you need more room, use the back of the page.

Scene	*What Mercutio says, does, or what others say about him*	*What this reveals about Mercutio's character*
Act II, scene i After the banquet, in the lane outside Capulet's orchard		
Act II, scene iv In the street when Benvolio informs him of Tybalt's challenge		
Act II, scene iv When he encounters the Nurse		

During-Reading Activity
for
Romeo and Juliet
Guide to Character Development: Nurse
Act II

Shakespeare reveals his characters in four ways:

ᵃ❧ through what the characters say to other characters in dialogue;

ᵃ❧ through what the characters reveal about their thoughts through long speeches to the audience called *soliloquies*;

ᵃ❧ through what other characters say about them;

ᵃ❧ through what they do, their actions.

As you read the play, examine the following scenes for what they reveal about the Nurse's character and fill in the chart briefly using your own words. If you need more room, use the back of the page.

Scene	*What the Nurse says, does, or what others say about her*	*What this reveals about the Nurse's character*
Act II, scene iv Nurse meets Romeo in the street		
Act II, scene v Nurse tells Juliet of Romeo's plans		

© 1993 by The Center for Applied Research in Education

NAME:_____   DATE:_____

Postreading Activity
for
Romeo and Juliet
Comprehension Check
Act II

Directions: After you've read all of Act II, use the following questions to check how well you've understood what you've read. For each question, select the most appropriate answer from the choices listed below it. Place the letter corresponding to your answer in the space to the left of the item number.

_____1. What promise does Juliet make to Romeo when they part at the end of the balcony scene, scene ii?

A. Never to see Romeo again.
B. To send Romeo a love letter.
C. To run away with him.
D. To send someone to find out about the wedding plans.
E. To come to see Romeo tomorrow night at his house.

_____2. When Romeo tells Friar Laurence that he's in love with Juliet, how does the friar react?

A. The friar is angry with Romeo.
B. The friar scolds Romeo but sees it as a way to resolve the feud.
C. The friar scolds Romeo for the impossible nature of the relationship.
D. The friar is happy for Romeo.
E. The friar is happy for Romeo but knows the relationship will never work.

_____3. Why does Juliet reject Romeo's offer to swear the truth of his love by the moon?

A. Because she doesn't believe in swearing.
B. Because she prefers the sun.
C. Because the moon sets at sunrise.
D. Because the moon is false.
E. Because she wants him to swear by something that is constant.

_____4. When the Nurse returns from her meeting with Romeo, why does she delay in telling Juliet about the wedding plans?

A. She's hungry and wants lunch first.
B. She wants to make sure that Lady Capulet isn't around to overhear them.
C. She has to beat Peter first.
D. She doesn't want Juliet to marry Romeo.
E. She's still angry and upset from the way that Mercutio treated her.

_____5. Which event suggests that the play might end unhappily?

A. Romeo and Juliet swear their undying love for each other.
B. Tybalt sends the letter to Romeo.
C. Nurse finds out the plans.
D. Romeo and Juliet marry.
E. Friar Laurence consents to marry Romeo and Juliet.

Postreading Activity
for
Romeo and Juliet
Small Group Discussion to Check Comprehension
Act II

Directions: After you've read all of Act II, in small groups, discuss each of the following questions briefly. Use the space below each question to note points you may want to share later. If you need more room, use the back of the page.

1. What promise does Juliet make to Romeo when they part at the end of the balcony scene, scene ii?

2. When Romeo tells Friar Laurence that he's in love with Juliet, how does the friar react?

3. Why does Juliet reject Romeo's offer to swear the truth of his love by the moon?

4. When the Nurse returns from her meeting with Romeo, why does she delay in telling Juliet about the wedding plans?

5. What events in Act II suggest that the play might end unhappily?

Postreading Activity
for
Romeo and Juliet
Critical Thinking Questions
Act II

Directions: To help develop your understanding of Act II, take time to think about and discuss these questions. The first question is the focus question and the point of the discussion. Don't be concerned that you may not be able to answer it at first. Proceed to the exploration questions and then return to the focus question.

Focus Question. Given the long-standing nature of the Montague-Capulet feud, why would you, as Romeo and Juliet do, be willing to risk either the love and protection of your family or your life to end it?

Exploration Questions.

1. What kinds of risks would you be willing to take in order to see someone of whom your family did not approve?

2. Given the feud between Romeo's family, the Montagues, and Juliet's, the Capulets, what risks and precautions does each take to see the other?

3. What types of risks and precautions have characters in other works that you've read had to take? What types of risk-taking does our society view as being beneficial? What types do we not condone?

4. Would you, like Romeo and Juliet, be willing to take the risks that they do in order to see each other? What other precautions might you take that they do not?

5. In other plays, stories, poems, or novels that you have read, what types of risks do the central characters take? Compare and contrast these risks with those of Romeo and Juliet.

6. Even if it meant disapproval from society, why would you be willing to risk seeing someone that the community felt you shouldn't?

© 1993 by The Center for Applied Research in Education

Postreading Activity
for
Romeo and Juliet
Language Exploration:
Figurative Language and Simile
Act II

Like other poets, Shakespeare explores abstract ideas—like love, honor, or justice—in his plays. To connect these ideas to his reader's experience, Shakespeare often compares an abstract idea to a more concrete example. When he does this, he speaks non-literally, using *figurative language*. As you continue to study *Romeo and Juliet*, you will have the opportunity to explore how Shakespeare uses language devices associated with figurative language: *simile, metaphor, personification,* and *apostrophe*.

One way to do this is to compare the two different terms using either *like* or *as*. This type of comparison is called *simile*. We continue to use similes in our daily speech. Consider these clichés:

ɛ

I am as hungry as a bear.
Angel runs like the wind.
The Barbarian ate like a pig.

ɛ

In the first example, the speaker can feel her own hunger but compares her appetite to a bear's to communicate it to others. In the second example, the physical act of Angel's running becomes powerful, energetic, and effortless like the wind. Using the comparison to a pig, the Barbarian's table manners leave much to be desired.

Directions: Similes are underlined in the following passages from scenes in Act II. Working in pairs, small groups, or as your teacher directs, review each passage in the context of the play and decide what the comparison suggests to the reader.

   1.   While Romeo watches Juliet on her balcony (scene ii), he supposes that her eyes are stars and how they would affect the appearance of her face:

ɛ

The brightness of her cheek would shame those stars,
As daylight doth a lamp;

ɛ

2. As Romeo (scene ii) continues to watch Juliet from afar and hears her sigh:

    ❧

    O, speak again, bright angel! <u>For thou art</u>
    <u>As glorious to this night</u>, being o'er my head,
    <u>As is a wingèd messenger of heaven</u>.

    ❧

3. Juliet (scene ii) reflecting upon having fallen in love with Romeo, her family's enemy:

    ❧

    What's in a name? That which we call <u>a rose</u>
    <u>By any other name would smell as sweet</u>.

    ❧

4. Juliet (scene ii) speaking to Romeo of his promise of true love:

    ❧

    I have no joy in <u>this contract</u> to-night.
    It <u>is</u> too rash, to unadvised, too sudden;
    <u>Too like lightning</u>, which doth cease to be
    Ere one can say it lightens.

    ❧

5. Juliet (scene ii) speaking to Romeo, wishing she could profess her love to him again and again:

ᶻ⅄

My <u>bounty is as boundless as the sea</u>,
My <u>love as deep</u>; the more I give to thee,

ᶻ⅄

6. Romeo (scene ii) commenting on Juliet calling him back after he's started to leave:

ᶻ⅄

It is my soul that calls upon my name.
How silver-sweet <u>sound lover's tongues by night</u>,
<u>Like softest music to attending ears</u>!

ᶻ⅄

7. Juliet to Romeo (scene ii):

ᶻ⅄

'Tis almost morning. I would have thee gone,—
And yet no further than <u>a wanton's bird</u>,
Who lets it hop a little from her hand,
<u>Like a poor prisoner in his twisted gyves</u>.

ᶻ⅄

8. Friar Laurence (scene iii) speaking about the dawn:

ঌ

And <u>fleckèd darkness like a drunkard reels</u>
<u>From forth day's path</u>. . .

ঌ

9. Juliet (scene v) complaining about the slowness of her Nurse in returning from meeting with Romeo:

ঌ

But <u>old folks</u>, many <u>fein as they were dead</u>—
Unwieldy, slow, heavy and pale as lead.

ঌ

10. The Nurse (scene v) complaining of her headache:

ঌ

Lord, how <u>my head aches</u>! What a head have I!
<u>It beats as if it would fall in twenty pieces</u>.

ঌ

NAME:_____   DATE:_____

Postreading Activity
for
Romeo and Juliet
Vocabulary in Context
Act II

Directions: In each of the passages below you will find one of the words from the prereading vocabulary list for Act II. Review the definitions given in the prereading vocabulary. Working individually, in pairs, or in small groups as your teacher directs, examine each of the underlined words in the following passages from Act II. For each word, use the appropriate meaning and develop a brief interpretation of the passage within the context of the play.

1. Mercutio (Act II, i) calling for Romeo who has slipped away:

   ≥∂

   The ape is dead, and I must <u>conjure</u> him.
   I <u>conjure</u> thee by Rosaline's bright eyes,
   By her high forehead, and her scarlet lip, ...

   ≥∂

2. Romeo (Act II, ii) comparing Juliet to the sun:

   ≥∂

   Arise fair sun and kill the <u>envious</u> moon,
   Who is already sick and pale with grief. . .

   ≥∂

3. Romeo (Act II, ii) responding to Juliet's fears of being caught:

   ≥∂

   Alack there lies more <u>peril</u> in thine eye
   Than twenty of their swords. . . .

   ≥∂

85

4. Juliet (Act II, ii) talking to Romeo:

    ❧

    Or if thou thinkest I am too quickly won,
    I'll frown and be <u>perverse</u>. . . .

    ❧

5. Juliet (Act II, ii) talking to Romeo:

    ❧

    If thy bent of love be honourable,
    Thy purpose marriage, send me word to-morrow,
    By one that I'll <u>procure</u> to come to thee. . . .

    ❧

6. Romeo (Act II, iii) asking Friar Laurence not to scold him for loving:

    ❧

    Thou <u>chid'st</u> me for loving Rosaline. . . .
    I pray thee <u>chide</u> me not . . . .

    ❧

7. Friar Laurence (Act II, iii) commenting to Romeo that something must cause him to be up early:

    ❧

    Young son, it argues a <u>distempered</u> head
    So soon to bid good morrow to thy bed. . . .

    ❧

© 1993 by The Center for Applied Research in Education

8. Romeo (Act II, iii) telling Friar Laurence where he's been:

       ❧

   I bear no hatred, blessed man; for lo,
   My <u>intercession</u> likewise steads my foe.

       ❧

9. Juliet (Act II, iii) speaking to Romeo:

       ❧

   Dost thou love me? I know thou wilt say ay,
   And I will take thy word; yet if thou swear'st,
   Thou mayst prove false; at lovers' <u>perjuries</u>
   They say Jove laughs.

       ❧

10. Juliet (Act II, v) complaining of the Nurse's slowness in returning with Romeo's wedding plans:

       ❧

    O she is lame, love's <u>heralds</u> should be thoughts,
    Which ten times faster glide than the sun's beams. . .

       ❧

NAME:_____ DATE:_____

Vocabulary Review Quiz
for
Romeo and Juliet
Act II

Directions: For each of the italicized words in the sentences below, determine which letter best reflects the use of the word in this context. Place the letter corresponding to your answer in the space to the left of the item number.

_____ 1. Juliet feels that thoughts should be the *heralds* of love.
In this context, *heralds* means

A. guardians B. counselors C. messenger D. predictors

_____ 2. Friar Laurence asks what *distempers* Romeo to cause him to be up so early.
In this context, *distempers* means

A. soothes B. disturbs C. awakens D. angers.

_____ 3. Friar Laurence *chides* Romeo for falling in and out of love so easily.
In this context, *chides* means

A. scolds B. hurts C. forgives D. banishes

_____ 4. Mercutio tries to *conjure* up Romeo by calling on Rosaline's spirit.
In this context, *conjure* means

A. to betray B. to look for C. to confuse D. to call by magic

_____ 5. Romeo feels the moon should be *envious* of the sun.
In this context, *envious* means

A. blinded by B. imitative C. concerned by D. jealous

_____ 6. Romeo feels marrying Juliet will be an *intercession* to end the feud between the two families.
In this context, *intercession* means

A. act of anger B. act of pleading C. act of penance
D. act of treason

_____ 7. By climbing into the Capulets' garden, Romeo puts his life in *peril*.
In this context, *peril* means

A. happiness B. safety C. trust D. danger

_____ 8. According to Juliet, lovers tell each other *perjuries*.
In this context, *perjuries* means

A. kind thoughts   B. dangers   C. lies   D. truths

_____ 9. In Shakespeare's time, young women, like Juliet or Rosaline, were expected to be *perverse*.
In this context, *perverse* means

A. contrary   B. angry   C. lonesome   D. happy

_____ 10. Juliet *procures* her Nurse to meet Romeo and learn of the plans for the marriage.
In this context, *procures* means

A. lies about   B. obtains easily   C. steals   D. obtains through effort

ACT III

NAME:_____   **DATE:**_____

Focusing Activities
for
Romeo and Juliet
Scenarios for Improvisation
Act III

Directions: Presented below are locations and situations involving characters. Before reading an individual scene, pretend to be one of the characters and act out the situation. Don't worry about speaking like characters in Shakespeare's play; just try to imagine how you would react to the situation and use your own language. Take a few minutes to discuss with the other performers what you would like to do. Be prepared to act out your scene for others in the class. Afterward, classmates outside your group may discuss what they've seen.

scene i. *Scene:* The public square in Verona, immediately following the wedding ceremony.

Characters: Tybalt and Romeo.

Situation: Tybalt wants revenge upon Romeo for crashing the family banquet. Romeo has just secretly married into the Capulet family, so he is happy and doesn't want to fight with his new cousin-in-law. Improvise the dialogue between these two.

scene ii. *Scene:* Juliet's bedroom.

Characters: Juliet and the Nurse.

Situation: Juliet is impatient for Romeo to come to her. The Nurse interrupts with bad news for her about Tybalt and Romeo. What does the Nurse say and how does Juliet respond?

Focusing Activities
for
Romeo and Juliet
Small Group Discussion Questions
Act III

Directions: Before reading scenes in Act III, discuss the questions in small groups. You may wish to make notes about your discussion, so you can share them with classmates or refer back to them after you've read the scene.

scene i.

1. At the end of Act II, Friar Laurence marries Romeo and Juliet, hoping to end the feud between the Capulets and Montagues. What seems to be a happy ending has occurred prior to the middle of the play. Let's take a look at the few lines from the prologue:

   ❧

   From forth the fatal loins of these two foes,
   A pair of star-crossed lovers take their life:
   Whose misadventured piteous overthrows
   Doth with their death bury their parents' strife.

   ❧

   From these lines, what do you think will happen to Romeo and Juliet? Whom do you think will be involved to bring about the unhappy ending that the prologue predicts?

2. In Act I, scene v (the party at the Capulets) Tybalt, Lady Capulet's hot-headed nephew, recognizes Romeo and informs Lord Capulet angrily that Romeo and his friends have crashed the party. Capulet orders Tybalt to remain calm; however, Tybalt grows sullen. What do you think Tybalt will do to counter the insult?

© 1993 by The Center for Applied Research in Education

scene ii.   How do you think Juliet will react when she learns that Romeo, now her husband, killed Tybalt, her cousin and closest relative aside from her parents? What new problems does Tybalt's death present for Romeo and Juliet?

scene iii.   How do you think Romeo will react to being banished?

scene iv.   How might the death of Tybalt affect Paris' desire to marry Juliet?

scene v.   How do you think Juliet will respond to her father's will that she marry Paris?

Focusing Activities
for
Romeo and Juliet
Speculation Journal
Act III

Directions: This activity will help you become involved actively with reading the play by helping you to determine a definite purpose for reading. Before you read these scenes in Act III, take a few minutes to respond in writing to the questions below. Don't worry about correct answers here. Use your own experience or what you have read in the play to speculate about what you think will happen. After reading a scene you may find that characters reacted differently than you thought. Don't worry about these differences; just make note of them because you will have opportunities to share these differences in other activities.

scene i.   Suppose Romeo, on his way home from marrying Juliet, meets Tybalt, who has sworn revenge upon Romeo for crashing the party. Now that Romeo has married Juliet secretly, what do you think Romeo will do and how might Tybalt react?

scene ii.   How do you think Juliet will react to the news that Romeo has killed Tybalt and has been banished?

scene iii.   What do you think Romeo will do when he learns that the Prince has banished him for killing Tybalt?

© 1993 by The Center for Applied Research in Education

scene iv.   What effect do you think Tybalt's death will have upon Capulet's interest that Juliet marry Paris?

scene v.   How do you think Juliet will react to her father's news that he wants her to marry Paris?

After Reading Act III: Now that you have finished reading the act, which of your speculations were most accurate? How do you account for them? Which ones were least like the action of the play? Why do you think you speculated as you did?

Prereading Activity
for
Romeo and Juliet
Vocabulary
Act III

Directions: Shakespeare uses the following words in Act III. The section below provides a brief definition of each word and provides a sentence to illustrate its meaning.

Definitions.
scene i

1.   **abroad:**   (adv.) outdoors, outside of normal home or territory.
     Example: Owls fly *abroad* at night.

2.   **discover:**   (v.) to uncover, reveal, make known.
     Example: Through research, Bill *discovered* that Columbus didn't land in North America.

3.   **exile:**   (n.) prolonged separation from one's home or native country; (v.) to separate or expel from one's homeland.
     Example: With the fall of communism in Eastern Europe, many Rumanians returned home from *exile*.

scene ii

4.   **banish:**   (v.) to expel from a country or place by decree, to rid.
     Example: Suzanne *banished* her sadness by listening to lively music.

5.   **mangle:**   (v.) to spoil, disfigure, ruin, mar badly.
     Example: Dad *mangled* my bicycle when he ran over it accidentally.

6.   **naught:**   (adj.) wicked, ruined; (n.) nothing, zero.
     Example: Gloria's elaborate plans to cheat on the test came to *naught* when she failed anyway.

7.   **tributary:**   (adj.) furnishing or adding to aid; auxiliary, contributory.
     Example: College students work part-time jobs and use the *tributary* income towards their college expenses.

scene iii

8.   **purgatory:**   (n.) place of temporary punishment, Hell.
     Example: After I got into trouble at school, waiting for my parents to come home from the parent-teacher conference was

liketime spent in *purgatory* compared to being grounded for two weeks.

scene v

9. **fickle:** (adj.) changeable casually; whimsical or inconstant emotionally.

   Example: The spring weather was *fickle*; warm one day but cold the next.

10. **unaccus-tomed:** (adj.) unusual, not habitual.

    Example: I'm *unaccustomed* to arriving late for any appointment.

Prereading Activity
for
Romeo and Juliet
Plot Summaries
Act III

Directions: To help you better understand and follow Shakespeare's play, read the summary of specific scenes immediately before you begin to read the original. If you get lost during the scene, refer to the summary again.

Act III, scene i

Sunday afternoon, immediately following the wedding, Benvolio, Mercutio, and several of the Montague's servants are in the public square. Benvolio urges Mercutio to get out of the sun, for the Capulets are out, and Benvolio fears another fight. But Mercutio puts Benvolio down for wanting to run from a fight.

Tybalt and other Capulets appear. Tybalt and Mercutio both want to pick a fight with each other and begin to taunt each other. Benvolio urges them either to fight out of sight or settle the dispute by talking. It doesn't work, and Mercutio and Tybalt draw their swords as Romeo appears.

Romeo tries to stop the fight, stepping between them. Thrusting beneath Romeo's arm, Tybalt stabs Mercutio fatally and then runs away. Although Mercutio makes a great act of dying, his friends think he's "just acting." When Romeo and the others realize that Mercutio is dying, it is too late. They take him into a neighboring house, where he soon dies.

Meanwhile Romeo believes that he has lost his courage because of his love for Juliet and has caused his friend's death. When Tybalt appears, Romeo, enraged, draws his sword and kills him. Soon the Prince and his men begin approaching, so Romeo flees.

Benvolio explains to the Prince, the Capulets, and the Montagues what has happened. Lady Capulet demands Romeo's life for slaying Tybalt. The Prince decides that Romeo should be banished rather than put to death.

Act III, scene ii

Juliet waits for Romeo anxiously in her garden. The Nurse enters with the rope ladder crying "he's dead." At first Juliet thinks the Nurse means Romeo, but she discovers that Romeo has killed Tybalt and is to be banished. Juliet decides that Romeo's banishment is worse than news of the death of all her family. She sends the Nurse to find Romeo and have him come to say goodbye.

Act III, scene iii

Romeo, having sought sanctuary in Friar Laurence's cell, lies crying in the corner. Friar Laurence tells him that his sentence is banishment rather than death. Romeo, like Juliet, sees banishment as a more severe punishment because it will separate him from his wife. Romeo hides when the Nurse enters, but comes out of the corner when he learns that she has brought a message and a ring, as a token from Juliet. The friar scolds Romeo for his tears and tells him to go to Mantua, a neighboring city, and wait for an appropriate time to return when they can tell their families of the marriage and ask forgiveness of the Prince.

Act III, scene iv

After midnight early Monday morning, Capulet agrees to the marriage of Juliet to Paris on Thursday.

Act III, scene v

At dawn on Monday, Romeo slips out of Juliet's chamber and prepares to ride to Mantua. The Nurse enters, announcing that Lady Capulet is coming. The lovers part. Lady Capulet tells her daughter that she is to wed Paris on Thursday. Juliet refuses. When Lord Capulet enters and finds Juliet in tears, he thinks that she grieves for Tybalt. When Juliet refuses to marry Paris, Capulet threatens to drag her to the church or disown her, throwing her into the street to support herself.

After Juliet's parents storm out, the Nurse urges Juliet to go ahead and marry Paris. The Nurse points out that no one knows differently, and Romeo can't return to challenge the marriage. Juliet sends the Nurse to her parents, telling them that she has gone to Friar Laurence for confession and absolution. Instead, Juliet admits that she is going to the friar for advice.

Class Period:

CHARACTER ASSIGNMENTS FOR ORAL READING GROUPS

Romeo and Juliet

Session 5: Act III, scenes i and ii

Characters	*Group 1*	*Group 2*	*Group 3*	*Group 4*
Benvolio	___	___	___	___
Mercutio	___	___	___	___
Tybalt	___	___	___	___
Romeo	___	___	___	___
Citizens, Nurse	___	___	___	___
Prince	___	___	___	___
Lady Capulet	___	___	___	___
Juliet	___	___	___	___

102

Class Period:

CHARACTER ASSIGNMENTS FOR ORAL READING GROUPS
Romeo and Juliet

Session 6: Act III, scenes iii, iv, v

Characters	*Group 1*	*Group 2*	*Group 3*	*Group 4*
Friar Laurence	___	___	___	___
Romeo	___	___	___	___
Nurse	___	___	___	___
Lord Capulet (scene iv)	___	___	___	___
Lord Capulet (scene v)	___	___	___	___
Paris	___	___	___	___
Lady Capulet	___	___	___	___
Juliet	___	___	___	___

**During-Reading Activity
for
Romeo and Juliet
Character Diary 3**
Act III
Sunday Afternoon through Early Monday Morning

Directions: Use the space below to record your character's reactions to the events that occur in Act III of *Romeo and Juliet*. Remember to include a summary of events, explain how your character learned of them, and give your character's reactions to these events.

The Personal Diary of

_____
(character's name)

Sunday, July 20, 1597 (Act III, scenes i–iii)
Evening

_____

_____

_____

_____

_____

_____

_____

Monday, July 21, 1597 (Act III, scenes iv and v)
Morning

_____

_____

_____

_____

_____

_____

_____

© 1993 by The Center for Applied Research in Education

NAME:_____   DATE:_____

During-Reading Activity
for
Romeo and Juliet
Viewing Act III, scene v
The Second Balcony Scene

Directions: After you've read this scene, viewing a film or video version may help you better understand how the text translates into the characters' actions. Although you may want to keep your copy of the play handy, don't be surprised if the actors' script varies from yours. Film scripts often delete or reorder the lines of the play. You may want to note questions you want to ask your teacher afterwards. After viewing the scene, take a few minutes to respond to the questions below.

1. In contrast to the first balcony scene (Act II, scene ii), how has Romeo and Juliet's relationship changed? How do the actors' facial expressions, tones of voice, and gestures enhance Shakespeare's words?

2. What changes do you notice in Juliet's character and relationship to her parents in this scene? How do the actors' facial expressions, tones of voice, and gestures enhance Shakespeare's words?

During-Reading Activity
for
Romeo and Juliet
Guide to Character Development: Romeo
Act III

Shakespeare reveals his characters in four ways:

- through what the characters say to other characters in dialogue;
- through what the characters reveal about their thoughts through long speeches to the audience called *soliloquies*;
- through what other characters say about them;
- through what they do, their actions.

As you read the play, examine the following scenes for what they reveal about Romeo's character and fill in the chart briefly using your own words. If you need more room, use the back of the page.

Scene	What Romeo says, does, or what others say about him	What this reveals about Romeo's character
Act III, scene i Romeo encounters Tybalt and Mercutio arguing in the street		
Act III, scene iii Romeo takes refuge in Friar Laurence's cell		
Act III, scene v Romeo bids Juliet farewell		

During-Reading Activity
for
Romeo and Juliet
Guide to Character Development: Juliet
Act III

Shakespeare reveals his characters in four ways:

ᴊᴗ through what the characters say to other characters in dialogue;

ᴊᴗ through what the characters reveal about their thoughts through long speeches to the audience called *soliloquies*;

ᴊᴗ through what other characters say about them;

ᴊᴗ through what they do, their actions.

As you read the play, examine the following scenes for what they reveal about Juliet's character and fill in the chart briefly using your own words. If you need more room, use the back of the page.

Scene	What Juliet says, does, or what others say about her	What this reveals about Juliet's character
Act III, scene ii Juliet waits for Romeo and learns of Tybalt's death		
Act III, scene v Juliet bids farewell to Romeo		
Act III, scene v Lord Capulet tells Juliet she is to marry Paris		

During-Reading Activity
for
Romeo and Juliet
Guide to Character Development: Mercutio
Act III

Shakespeare reveals his characters in four ways:

- ❧ through what the characters say to other characters in dialogue;
- ❧ through what the characters reveal about their thoughts through long speeches to the audience called *soliloquies*;
- ❧ through what other characters say about them;
- ❧ through what they do, their actions

As you read the play, examine the following scenes for what it reveals about Mercutio's character and fill in the chart briefly using your own words. If you need more room, use the back of the page.

Scene	What Mercutio says, does, or what others say about him	What this reveals about Mercutio's character
Act III, scene i Mercutio meets Tybalt in the street		

NAME:_____   DATE:_____

During-Reading Activity
for
Romeo and Juliet
Guide to Character Development: Nurse
Act III

Shakespeare reveals his characters in four ways:

❧ through what the characters say to other characters in dialogue;

❧ through what the characters reveal about their thoughts through long speeches to the audience called *soliloquies*;

❧ through what other characters say about them;

❧ through what they do, their actions.

As you read the play, examine the following scenes for what they reveal about the Nurse's character and fill in the chart briefly using your own words. If you need more room, use the back of the page.

Scene	*What the Nurse says, does, or what others say about her*	*What this reveals about the Nurse's character*
Act III, scene ii Nurse tells Juliet of Tybalt's death		
Act III, scene iii Nurse meets Romeo in Friar Laurence's cell		
Act III, scene v Lord Capulet tells Juliet she will marry Paris		

Postreading Activity
for
Romeo and Juliet
Comprehension Check
Act III

Directions: After you've read all of Act III, use the following questions to check how well you've understood what you've read. For each question, select the most appropriate answer from the choices listed below it. Place the letter corresponding to your answer in the space to the left of the item number.

____1.   What sentence does the Prince give Romeo for the killing of Tybalt?

A. The Prince orders Romeo beheaded.
B. The Prince orders the deaths of both Lord Capulet and Lord Montague.
C. The Prince banishes Romeo.
D. The Prince banishes Romeo and Juliet.
E. The Prince exiles Juliet.

____2.   When Juliet's parents see her crying after Romeo's departure, how do they interpret her tears?

A. She is crying for happiness because she is to marry Paris.
B. She is crying for sadness because she is marrying Paris.
C. She is crying because she is being separated from Romeo.
D. She is crying because she is angry with Romeo.
E. She is crying because of the death of Tybalt.

____3.   What does Mercutio mean when he describes his wound from Tybalt with these lines?

ᐧᐧᐧ

No, 'tis not so deep as a well, nor so wide as a church door; but 'tis enough, 'twill serve. Ask for me to-morrow, and you shall find me a grave man.

ᐧᐧᐧ

A. His wound is minor.
B. His wound will kill him.
C. His wound needs washing.
D. His wound needs the attention of a priest.
E. His wound is serious but he will recover.

© 1993 by The Center for Applied Research in Education

_____ 4. In scene v, when Lady Capulet informs Juliet of the plans for her to marry Paris on Thursday, Juliet replies,

ع

I pray you tell my lord and father, madam,
I will not marry yet; and when I do, I swear
It shall be Romeo, whom you know I hate,
Rather than Paris.

ع

What does Juliet mean by these lines and how do her parents interpret them?

A. Juliet will marry Paris and refuse to recognize her marriage to Romeo.
B. Juliet refuses to marry Paris but will eventually marry Romeo publicly.
C. Juliet refuses to marry either Paris or Romeo.
D. Juliet will consent to marry only Paris.
E. Juliet will consent to marry only Romeo.

_____ 5. In Act III, scene v, Juliet asks the Nurse for advice about marrying Paris. The Nurse replies,

ع

        Romeo.
Is banished; and all the world to nothing,
That he dares ne'er come back to challenge you;
Or if he do, it needs must be by stealth.
Then since the case so stands as now it doth,
I think it best you married with the county.
O, he's a lovely gentleman.
Romeo's a dishclout to him; an eagle, madam,
Hath not so green, so quick, so fair an eye
As Paris hath. Beshrew my very heart,
I think you are happy in this second match,
For it excels your first; or if it did not,
Your first is dead—or 'twere as good he were
As living here, and you no use of him.

ع

© 1993 by The Center for Applied Research in Education

111

In these lines, which reason does the Nurse *not* use to try to persuade Juliet to go ahead and marry Paris?

A. She implies Paris is more handsome than Romeo.
B. Romeo is as good as dead.
C. Paris is wealthier than Romeo.
D. Romeo cannot return to challenge the marriage publicly.
E. She compares Romeo to a dishcloth and Paris to an eagle.

Postreading Activity
for
Romeo and Juliet
Small Group Discussion to Check Comprehension
Act III

Directions: After you've read all of Act III, in small groups, discuss each of the following questions briefly. Use the space below each question to note points you may wish to share later. If you need more room, use the back of the page.

1. What sentence does the Prince give Romeo for the killing of Tybalt?

2. When Juliet's parents see her crying after Romeo's departure, how do they interpret her tears?

3. What does Mercutio mean when he describes his wound from Tybalt with these lines?

ข

No, tis not so deep as a well, nor so wide as a church door; but 'tis enough, 'twill serve. Ask for me to-morrow, and you shall find me a grave man.

ข

4. In scene v, when Lady Capulet informs Juliet of the plans for her to marry Paris on Thursday, Juliet replies,

ک

I pray you tell my lord and father, madam,
I will not marry yet; and when I do, I swear
It shall be Romeo, whom you know I hate,
Rather than Paris.

ک

How does what Juliet mean by her reply differ from how her parents interpret it?

5. How does the Nurse's advice to Juliet about marrying Paris differ from her own vow at the end of the act?

NAME:_____   DATE:_____

Postreading Activity
for
Romeo and Juliet
Critical Thinking Questions
Act III

Directions: To help develop your understanding of Act III, take time to think about and discuss these questions. The first question is the focus question and the point of the discussion. Don't be concerned that you may not be able to answer it at first. Proceed to the exploration questions and then return to the focus question.

Focus Question. If Juliet were a friend of yours today, what advice would you give her at the end of Act III?

Exploration Questions.

1. Compare Juliet's reactions to her parents' news that she marry Paris in both Act I, scene iii and Act III, scene v. How do you account for the differences in Juliet's responses?

2. In other works of literature that you've read, how have the characters sought revenge against others?

3. In what situations would you act differently either to maintain your reputation or to keep up appearances?

4. To what extent do you think Mercutio's and Tybalt's fighting is motivated by revenge and to what extent do you think it is motivated by their desires to maintain their reputations as excellent swordsmen?

5. When you act to maintain a reputation or receive attention, how do your peers react? How do adults who may observe your actions react?

6. If you lived in a society where you were dependent upon your parents totally, as Juliet is, what circumstances would cause you to risk being thrown out of the house and have society scorn you as an ungrateful child?

Postreading Activity
for
Romeo and Juliet
Language Exploration:
Metaphor
Act III

Metaphor is another language device associated with figurative language. Like *similes* that you studied in Act II, metaphors also compare two ideas. Usually, one idea tends to be concrete while the other tends to be abstract. Where a simile points out the comparison using *like* or *as*, a metaphor makes the comparison directly. Consider these examples of the same comparison stated as both simile and metaphor:

Simile:	Sam is as hungry as a bear.
Metaphor:	When Sam is hungry, he's a real bear.
Simile:	Angel runs like the wind.
Metaphor:	Angel breezed across the finish line to win the relay.
Simile:	The Barbarian ate like a pig.
Metaphor:	The Barbarian is a real pig when he eats.

Directions: Metaphors are underlined in the following passages from scenes in Act III. Working in pairs, small groups, or as your teacher directs, review each passage in the context of the play and decide what the comparison suggests to the reader.

1. Juliet (scene ii) wanting night to come, so she and Romeo can be together:

ᘒ

Come, civil night,
Thou sober suited matron, all in black.

ᘒ

2. Juliet (scene ii) describing Romeo's face to her Nurse:

ᘒ

Upon his brow shame is ashamed to sit
For 'tis a throne where honor may be

ᘒ

© 1993 by The Center for Applied Research in Education

3. Juliet (scene ii) telling her Nurse that she has dishonored Romeo:

❧

Back, foolish tears, back to your native spring!
Your tributary drops belong to woe.

❧

4. Romeo (scene iii) reflects to Friar Laurence upon the hellish punishment banishment from Verona will be:

❧

Heaven is here,
Where Juliet lives.

❧

5. Romeo (scene iii) continues to reflect upon his banishment:

❧

Flies may do this but I must fly
They are freemen, but I am banishèd.

❧

6. Friar Laurence (scene iii) tries to comfort Romeo:

❧

I'll give thee armor to keep off that word [banishment];
Adversity's sweet milk, philosophy

❧

117

7.   Friar Laurence (scene iii) comforting Romeo:

❧

The <u>law</u>, that threatened death, <u>becomes thy friend</u>
And turns it to exile.

❧

8.   Romeo (scene v) speaking to Juliet:

❧

It was <u>the lark</u>, <u>the herald of the morn</u>

❧

9.   Romeo (scene v) calling Juliet's attention to the sunrise:

❧

Look, love, <u>what envious streaks</u>
<u>Do lace the severing clouds in yonder East</u>.

❧

10. Lord Capulet (scene v) comments upon Juliet's eyes that are red from crying:

❧

For still thy eyes, <u>which I may call the sea</u>,
<u>Do ebb and flow with tears</u>;

❧

NAME:_____   DATE:_____

**Postreading Activity
for
Romeo and Juliet
Vocabulary in Context
Act III**

Directions: In each of the passages below you will find one of the words from the prereading vocabulary list for Act III. Review the definitions given in the prereading vocabulary. Working individually, in pairs, or in small groups as your teacher directs, examine each of the underlined words in the following passages from Act III. For each word, use the appropriate meaning and develop a brief interpretation of the passage within the context of the play.

1. Benvolio (III, i) asking Mercutio and the others to go inside:

ક

*I pray thee good Mercutio, let's retire.
The day is hot, the Capulets <u>abroad</u>;*

ક

2. Benvolio (III, i) explaining the deaths of Mercutio and Tybalt to the Prince:

ક

*O noble Prince, I can <u>discover</u> all
The unlucky manage of this fatal brawl.*

ક

3. Prince (III, i) sentencing Romeo:

119

❧

And for that offense
Immediately we do <u>exile</u> him hence.

❧

4. Nurse (III, ii) telling Juliet of the death of Tybalt:

❧

Tybalt is gone, and Romeo <u>banished</u>.

❧

5. Juliet (III, ii) defending Romeo:

❧

Shall I speak ill of him that is my husband?
Oh poor my lord, what tongue shall smooth thy name,
When I, thy three-hours wife have <u>mangled</u> it?

❧

6. Nurse (III, ii) commenting upon the death of Tybalt and Romeo's banishment:

❧

There's no trust,
No faith, no honesty in men; all perjured,
All forsworn, all <u>naught</u>, all dissemblers.

❧

7. Juliet (III, ii) realizing she needs to weep for Romeo's banishment:

    ❧

    Back foolish tears, back to your native spring,
    Your <u>tributary</u> drops belong to woe.

    ❧

8. Romeo (III, iii) responding to his banishment:

    ❧

    There is no world without Verona walls,
    But <u>purgatory</u>, torture, hell itself.

    ❧

9. Juliet (III, v) commenting on Romeo's banishment:

    ❧

    Be <u>fickle</u>, fortune;
    For then I hope thou will not keep him long,
    But send him back.

    ❧

10. Juliet (III, v) commenting on her mother's rising early:

    ❧

    Is she not down so late, or up so early?
    What <u>unaccustomed</u> cause procures her hither?

    ❧

121

Vocabulary Review Quiz
for
Romeo and Juliet
Act III

© 1993 by The Center for Applied Research in Education

Directions: For each of the italicized words in the sentences below, determine which letter best reflects the use of the word in this context. Place the letter corresponding to your answer in the space to the left of the item number.

_____1.   For Juliet, Tybalt's death is *tributary* to her sorrow of having Romeo banished.
In this context, *tributary* means

A. secondary   B. contributory   C. absent   D. deleting

_____2.   By not defending Romeo as a murderer, Juliet feels that she has *mangled* the character of her husband.
In this context, *mangled* means

A. praised   B. marred badly   C. lied about   D. confused

_____3.   Benvolio seems to *discover* the start of many of the street fights for the Prince.
In this context, *discover* means

A. uncover   B. instigate   C. investigate   D. reveal

_____4.   The Prince *banishes* Romeo for killing Tybalt.
In this context, *banishes* means

A. expels   B. soften   C. murders   D. executes

_____5.   For Romeo any time away from Juliet is *purgatory*.
In this context, *purgatory* means

A. a prison   B. death sentence   C. place of reflection
D. place of torment

_____6.   The Nurse feels that all men are *naught* when Romeo slays her friend Tybalt.
In this context, *naught* means

A. trustworthy   B. serious   C. wicked   D. simple-minded

_____7. According to Friar Laurence's plan, once everyone thinks Juliet is dead, she can join Romeo in *exile*.
In this context, *exile* means
A. prison   B. honeymoon   C. brief vacation
D. prolonged separation from home

_____8. At the beginning of the play, Romeo seems *fickle* by falling in and out of love so easily.
In this context, *fickle* means
A. casually changeable   B. sad   C. lonely   D. lost

_____9. Benvolio warns Mercutio that the Capulets are *abroad* and looking for a fight.
In this context, *abroad* means
A. angry   B. roaming the streets   C. at home   D. on vacation

_____10. Juliet notices that her mother is *unaccustomed* to rising early.
In this context, *unaccustomed* means
A. unwelcomed   B. serious   C. usual   D. not habitual

ACT IV

NAME:_____   DATE:_____

Focusing Activities
for
Romeo and Juliet
Scenarios for Improvisation
Act IV

Directions: Presented below are locations and situations involving characters. Before reading an individual scene, pretend to be one of the characters and act out the situation. Don't worry about speaking like characters in Shakespeare's play; just try to imagine how you would react to the situation and use your own language. Take a few minutes to discuss with the other performers what you would like to do. Be prepared to act out your scene for others in the class. Afterward, classmates outside your group may discuss what they've seen.

scene i.   *Scene:* Friar Laurence's cell.

Characters: Friar Laurence and Juliet.

Situation: Juliet has come to Friar Laurence to make her confession supposedly but more importantly to seek his advice. What help does she ask of him and what advice and help does he give her?

scene ii.   *Scene:* The Capulets' house.

Characters: Lord Capulet and Juliet.

Situation: Juliet returns from her visit to Friar Laurence. She goes to her father, wishing to make peace with him. What does she tell him and how does he reply?

Focusing Activities
for
Romeo and Juliet
Small Group Discussion Questions
Act IV

Directions: Before reading the scenes in Act IV, discuss the questions in small groups. You may wish to make notes about your discussion, so you can share them with classmates or refer back to them after you've read the scene.

scene i. Friar Laurence has sent Romeo away to Mantua, promising to send messages by Balthasar. Juliet has decided to seek the assistance of the friar as well. What do you think Friar Laurence may do to help Romeo and Juliet be together?

scene ii. Juliet knows that her father is angry with her. How do you think she can convince him that she will be obedient to his will without giving away her plans to be with Romeo?

scene iii. If you were Juliet, what doubts might you have about Friar Laurence's potion before you drank it?

scenes iv and v. Based upon what you've seen of Lord and Lady Capulet and the Nurse, what moods do you think each would be in on Thursday morning when Juliet is to marry Paris? What do you think will happen with all the preparations for the wedding feast?

© 1993 by The Center for Applied Research in Education

NAME:_____   DATE:_____

Focusing Activities
for
Romeo and Juliet
Speculation Journal
Act IV

Directions: This activity will help you become involved actively with reading the play by helping you to determine a definite purpose for reading. Before you read these scenes in Act IV, take a few minutes to respond in writing to the questions below. Don't worry about correct answers here. Use your own experience or what you have read in the play to speculate about what you think will happen. After reading a scene you may find that characters reacted differently than you thought. Don't worry about these differences; just make note of them because you will have opportunities to share these differences in other activities.

scene i. How do you think Friar Laurence might use his position as a priest and his knowledge of plants to help Juliet?

scene ii. What do you think Juliet will do to seek her father's forgiveness without giving away the Friar's plan for her to be with Romeo?

scene iii. The night before Juliet is to marry Paris, she will drink the strange potion that Friar Laurence has given her. What thoughts do you think might cross her mind before she drinks the potion?

scenes
iv and v. What are members of the Capulet household expecting for Juliet's wedding day and how do you think they will respond if they can't awaken Juliet?

After
Reading
Act IV: Now that you have finished reading the act, which of your speculations were most accurate? How do you account for them? Which ones were least like the action of the play? Why do you think you speculated as you did?

**Prereading Activity
for
Romeo and Juliet
Vocabulary
*Act IV***

Directions: Shakespeare uses the following words in Act IV. The section below provides a brief definition of each word and provides a sentence to illustrate its meaning.

Definitions.

scene i

1. **entreat:** (v.) to ask for sincerely, beg, implore.
   Example: Pamela *entreated* her mother for a new prom dress.

2. **immoder- ately:** (adv.) excessively; beyond reasonable boundaries, without bounds.
   Example: Great-grandmother was tidy *immoderately,* for she combed the fringe on the rugs each morning.

3. **pensive:** (adj.) expressing thoughtfulness or sadness; reflective; meditative.
   Example: After reading about Robin Hood, the *pensive* boy imagined his own adventures against the Sheriff of Nottingham.

4. **prorogue:** (v.) to prolong or postpone; to discontinue.
   Example: On April 14, we knew we couldn't *prorogue* doing our income taxes any longer because the deadline was the next night.

5. **resort:** (v.) to have ability to use as a final resource; to go to frequently or regularly.
   Example: When I visit my relatives in Georgia, I *resort* to a Southern accent, so I can communicate with them.

6. **wane:** (v.) to decrease in intensity; to lessen to bring to an end.
   Example: The runner's strength *waned*, causing him to collapse before he finished the race.

scene ii

7. **cunning:** (adj.) showing or made with great skill; skillful
   Example: David was a *cunning* hunter.

8. **prostrate:** (v.) to throw oneself face down on the ground in humility.
   (adj.) lying flat or full length as on the ground.
   Example: The peasant *prostrated* himself before the king to beg for mercy.

scene iii

9. **cull:** (v.) to choose, select; gather the choice parts from.
   Example: Steve *culled* all the red M & M's from the entire bowl.

10. **stifle:** (v.) to smother; to suppress or curb.
    Example: David *stifled* the creativity of the decorations committee when he insisted it only accept his suggestions.

NAME:_____   DATE:_____

Prereading Activity
for
Romeo and Juliet
Plot Summaries
Act IV

Directions: To help you better understand and follow Shakespeare's play, read the summary of specific scenes immediately before you begin to read the original. If you get lost during the scene, refer to the summary again.

Act IV,
scene i

In Friar Laurence's cell on Monday, Paris comes to discuss with Friar Laurence the arrangements of the Thursday wedding. Juliet interrupts and pretends to have come to make confession. Because the confession needs to be heard in private, Paris plans to leave but first asks Juliet to "confess" that she loves him. Juliet phrases her responses to Paris cleverly so she remains true to Romeo while Paris presumes Juliet's love is directed towards him.

Friar Laurence tells Juliet that he knows of her grief—the death of her cousin, the desperation about Romeo, and the plans for her to marry Paris. Juliet wants a plan from the priest to prevent the marriage or she says she will kill herself. The friar recognizes that Juliet is indeed desperate enough to kill herself although he warns her that doing so would bring everlasting damnation to her soul. He develops a plan.

He gives her a potion made from the plants and herbs that he gathers. The friar tells Juliet to take it when she retires the night before the wedding. The potion will put her into a 42-hour sleep, but will make her family think that she is dead. The friar believes Juliet will take the potion Wednesday night and awaken Friday evening. The plan will give him two days to get the letter to Romeo. Once Juliet's family has buried her in the family tomb, Friar Laurence will come for her on Friday evening and help her escape to Mantua, where she can be with Romeo.

Act IV,
scene ii

Meanwhile, all of the Capulet household is making preparations for the wedding feast. Capulet is pleased that Juliet has gone to confession. When she returns, she asks her father to forgive her and he does, thinking that she has agreed to marry Paris. Because of Lord Capulet's joy, he immediately decides to move the wedding ahead one day to Wednesday. Juliet asks the Nurse to help her select a dress to wear the next day.

Act IV, *scene iii*	Tuesday night, Juliet and the Nurse are in the process of selecting a dress for the wedding that Lord Capulet has moved to Wednesday. Lady Capulet enters and asks if they need any help. When Juliet says no, her mother and the Nurse leave. Juliet relates her fears in the long soliloquy. She says farewell to her family and is tempted to call them back. She wonders if the potion will work or whether it will poison her, for Friar Laurence might want her out of the way so he won't get into trouble for their marriage. She decides that the friar can be trusted after all. But then she speculates upon what will happen to her if she isn't rescued from the tomb. Will she die in there, be attacked by the ghosts, or simply go mad and kill herself anyway? She takes the potion and falls onto her bed.
Act IV, *scene iv*	During the night, the whole household continues making preparations for the wedding. At dawn on Wednesday, Capulet sends the Nurse to awaken Juliet for her wedding day.
Act IV, *scene v*	When the Nurse enters, she accuses Juliet of being lazy and wanting to stay in bed. When she shakes Juliet, she thinks that the girl is dead and alerts the entire household. Lady Capulet, Lord Capulet, and Paris all mourn for Juliet. Finally Friar Laurence enters and consoles the family, reminding them to rejoice, for Juliet's soul is in heaven. What was to be a day of celebration becomes a day of mourning.

Class Period:

CHARACTER ASSIGNMENTS FOR ORAL READING GROUPS

Romeo and Juliet

Session 7: Act IV, scenes i, ii, iii, iv, v

Characters	*Group 1*	*Group 2*	*Group 3*	*Group 4*
Friar Laurence	_____	_____	_____	_____
Musicians/Fellows	_____	_____	_____	_____
Paris, Peter	_____	_____	_____	_____
Juliet	_____	_____	_____	_____
Lord Capulet	_____	_____	_____	_____
Servant	_____	_____	_____	_____
Nurse	_____	_____	_____	_____
Lady Capulet	_____	_____	_____	_____

135

**During-Reading Activity
for
Romeo and Juliet
Character Diary 4**
*Act IV
Monday, Tuesday, Wednesday Morning*

Directions: Use the space below to record your character's reactions to the events
that occur in Act IV of *Romeo and Juliet*. Remember to include a summary
of events, explain how your character learned of them, and give your
character's reactions to these events. Because the act contains five scenes,
you may wish to record your character's entries as you read each scene.
If you need additional room, use the back of this sheet.

The Personal Diary of

_____
(character's name)

Monday, July 21, 1597 (Act IV, scenes i–ii)

_____

_____

_____

Tuesday, July 22, 1597 (Act IV, scene iii)

_____

_____

_____

_____

Wednesday, July 23, 1597 (Act IV, scenes iv and v)
Late morning/early afternoon

_____

_____

_____

_____

NAME:_____   DATE:_____

During-Reading Activity
for
Romeo and Juliet
Viewing Act IV, scene i
Juliet Meets Paris at Friar Laurence's Cell

Directions: After you've read this scene, viewing a film or video version may help you better understand how the text translates into the characters' actions. Although you may want to keep your copy of the play handy, don't be surprised if the actors' script varies from yours. Film scripts often delete or reorder the lines in the play. You may want to note questions you want to ask your teacher afterwards. After viewing the scene, take a few minutes to respond to the questions below.

1. When Paris meets Juliet outside Friar Laurence's cell, how does he interpret what Juliet says differently from what Juliet says? How do the actors' facial expressions, tones of voice, and gestures enhance Shakespeare's words?

2. What seems to be Juliet's emotional state when she first enters Friar Laurence's cell? How and why has she changed by the end of the scene? How does the visual version of this scene differ from the impressions you had when you first read it?

During-Reading Activity
for
Romeo and Juliet
Guide to Character Development: Juliet
Act IV

Shakespeare reveals his characters in four ways:

ॐ through what the characters say to other characters in dialogue;

ॐ through what the characters reveal about their thoughts through long speeches to the audience called *soliloquies*;

ॐ through what other characters say about them;

ॐ through what they do, their actions.

As you read the play, examine the following scenes for what they reveal about Juliet's character and fill in the chart briefly using your own words. If you need more room, use the back of the page.

Scene	*What Juliet says, does, or what others say about her*	*What this reveals about Juliet's character*
Act IV, scene i Juliet meets with Friar Laurence		
Act IV, scene iii Juliet and Nurse select a dress for her wedding and she takes potion		

© 1993 by The Center for Applied Research in Education

During-Reading Activity
for
Romeo and Juliet
Guide to Character Development: Nurse
Act IV

Shakespeare reveals his characters in four ways:

- through what the characters say to other characters in dialogue;

- through what the characters reveal about their thoughts through long speeches to the audience called *soliloquies*;

- through what other characters say about them;

- through what they do, their actions.

As you read the play, examine the following scenes for what they reveal about the Nurse's character and fill in the chart briefly using your own words. If you need more room, use the back of the page.

Scene	What the Nurse says, does, or what others say about her	What this reveals about the Nurse's character
Act IV, scene iii Juliet prepares for her wedding to Paris		
Act IV, scene v Nurse discovers Juliet's body		

Postreading Activity
for
Romeo and Juliet
Comprehension Check
Act IV

Directions: After you've read all of Act IV, use the following questions to check how well you've understood what you've read. For each question, select the most appropriate answer from the choices listed below it. Place the letter corresponding to your answer in the space to the left of the item number.

_____1. What solution does Friar Laurence propose to help Juliet avoid marrying Paris?

A. That Juliet kill herself.
B. That she flee to join Romeo immediately.
C. That she drink the potion that he gives her.
D. That she marry Paris.
E. That she forget about Romeo.

_____2. When Juliet returns from seeing Friar Laurence, why does Lord Capulet think Juliet has consented to marry Paris?

A. Because she has recovered from the death of Tybalt.
B. Because she says she will marry Paris.
C. Because she says that she hates Romeo for killing Tybalt.
D. Because she begs forgiveness from him.
E. Because she has run into Paris at Friar Laurence's cell.

_____3. When Juliet goes to Friar Laurence's cell, she meets Paris. Although Paris speaks of their marriage, how does Juliet reply?

A. Her answers refer equally to her marriage to Romeo.
B. She avoids the issue and discusses the weather.
C. She scolds Paris for raising the issue.
D. She lies to Paris that she is excited at the prospect of marrying him.
E. She says nothing but hurries in to see Friar Laurence.

_____ 4. Before taking the potion, why does Juliet lay out a dagger on her bed?

A. So her family will think she stabbed herself.
B. So she can kill herself in case the potion doesn't work.
C. So Romeo can kill himself when he comes.
D. So she can kill Paris in the morning.
E. So her family can kill themselves when they discover her body.

_____ 5. What does Juliet *not* fear in these lines from Act IV, scene iii?

ᏋᏋ

How if when I am laid into the tomb,
I wake before the time that Romeo
Come to redeem me? There's a fearful point!
Shall I not then be stifled in the vault,
To whose foul mouth no healthsome air breathes in,
And there die strangled ere my Romeo comes?

. . .

Alack, alack, is it not like that I,
So early waking—what with loathsome smells,
And shrieks like mandrakes torn out of the earth,
That living mortals, hearing them, run mad—
O, if I wake, shall I not be distraught,
Environed with all these hideous fears,
And madly play with my forefathers' joints,
And pluck the mangled Tybalt from his shroud,
And in this rage, with some great kinsman's bone
As with a club dash out my desp'rate brains?

ᏋᏋ

A. Suffocating if she awakens before Romeo comes.
B. Going insane.
C. Beating her brains out.
D. Stabbing Tybalt's body.
E. Playing insanely with the bones of some ancestor.

Postreading Activity
for
Romeo and Juliet
Small Group Discussion to Check Comprehension
Act IV

Directions: After you've read all of Act IV in small groups, discuss each of the following questions briefly. Use the space below each question to note points you may want to share later. If you need more room, use the back of the page.

1. What solution does Friar Laurence propose to help Juliet avoid marrying Paris?

2. Why does Capulet think Juliet has consented to marry Paris?

3. When Juliet goes to Friar Laurence's cell, she meets Paris. Although Paris speaks of their marriage, how does Juliet reply?

4. Before taking the potion, why does Juliet lay out a dagger on her bed?

5. Evaluate Friar Laurence's plan to help Juliet.

NAME:_____   DATE:_____

Postreading Activity
for
Romeo and Juliet
Critical Thinking Questions
Act IV

Directions: To help develop your understanding of Act IV, take time to think about and discuss these questions. The first question is the focus question and the point of the discussion. Don't be concerned that you may not be able to answer it at first. Proceed to the exploration questions and then return to the focus question.

Focus Question.   If Juliet were alive today, how would you attempt to put aside some of her fears about taking the potion? How would you help her accept those fears that couldn't be put aside?

Exploration Questions.

1.   Why is Juliet afraid to take the potion at first? What assurances does Friar Laurence give her that the potion will work?

2.   What situations in life or other works of literature that you've read would make you or the character desperate enough to consume an unknown drug in order to escape?

3.   If you were Juliet, why would you be willing to follow Friar Laurence's plan? If you wouldn't, what other plan would you devise?

4.   In what ways are Juliet's fears of the potion similar to or different from the reactions of characters or people that you've known dealing with serious problems?

5.   Caught in a similar situation to Juliet's, what fears might you express and what solution would you seek?

6.   It's normal for us to fear the unknown, especially death. What fears do you or people your own age have about death or experiences with death?

143

NAME:_____ DATE:_____

Postreading Activity
for
Romeo and Juliet
Language Exploration:
Personification
Act IV

One evening you are watching television and your family dog is dozing on the floor, feet outstretched. The dog's feet begin to move, and it barks softly but remains asleep. Your parents smile and point out that the dog is dreaming about chasing cars.

In the middle of your mathematics exam, the batteries go dead on your calculator. You put it away in disgust, saying "this machine is out to get me."

You've probably heard someone say "Love is blind." The cliché suggests anyone who is in love is unable to see his or her lover's faults.

In each of these examples, people have given human qualities to nonhuman things. From the evidence of watching the dog, we presume that the dog is dreaming. Similarly, the episode with the calculator presumes that the machine will react like human beings, the calculator wants revenge. In literature, authors often give human qualities to nonhuman things. This technique is called *personification*.

Directions: The following underlined passages from Acts I–IV are examples of personification. Working in pairs, small groups, or as your teacher directs, try reordering these lines. Once you've written your results, go back to the scene and look at the lines in context.

1. Lord Montague (Act I, scene i) describing Romeo's wandering about before sunrise:

   &

   But all so soon as the all-cheering sun
   Should in the farthest East begin to draw
   The shady curtains from Aurora's bed,

   &

2. Lord Capulet (Act I, scene ii) speaking about the coming of spring:

   &

   When well appareled April on the heel
   Of limping Winter treads

   &

© 1993 by The Center for Applied Research in Education

3.   Romeo (Act II, scene ii) speaking of Juliet:

ઢ

Arise fair sun and kill the envious moon

ઢ

4.   Juliet (Act II, scene ii) speaking to Romeo:

ઢ

bondage is hoarse and may not speak aloud

ઢ

5.   Friar Laurence (Act II, scene iii) describing the sun rise:

ઢ

The grey-eyed morn smiles on frowning night,
Check'ring the Eastern clouds with streaks of light.

ઢ

6.   Friar Laurence (Act III, scene iii) comforting Romeo who has been banished:

ઢ

Happiness courts thee in her best array

ઢ

145

7. Romeo (Act III, scene v) describing the sunrise to Juliet before he leaves her:

&

Night's candles are burnt out, and <u>jocund day</u>
<u>Stands tiptoe on the misty mountain tops</u>

&

8. Lord Capulet (Act IV, scene v) commenting upon Juliet's "death:"

&

<u>Death is my son-in-law, Death is my heir</u>

&

9. Lady Capulet (Act IV, scene v) responding to Juliet's "death:"

&

Most miserable hour that <u>e'er time saw</u>
<u>In lasting labor of his pilgrimage!</u>

&

10. Friar Laurence (Act IV, scene v) trying to console Lord and Lady Capulet:

&

For though fond <u>nature bids us all lament</u>
<u>Yet nature's tears are reason's merriment.</u>

&

© 1993 by The Center for Applied Research in Education

NAME:________________________________ DATE:________________

Postreading Activity
for
Romeo and Juliet
Vocabulary in Context
Act IV

Directions: In each of the passages below you will find one of the words from the prereading vocabulary list for Act IV. Review the definitions given in the prereading vocabulary. Working individually, in pairs, or in small groups as your teacher directs, examine each of the underlined words in the following passages from Act IV. For each word, use the appropriate meaning and develop a brief interpretation of the passage within the context of the play.

1. Friar Laurence (IV, i) requesting time alone with Juliet from Paris:

   My lord, we must entreat the time alone.

2. Paris (IV, i) speaking of Juliet:

   Immoderately she weeps for Tybalt's death
   And therefore have I little talked of love. . .

3. Friar Laurence (IV, i) to Juliet, who has come to make confession:

   My leisure serves me pensive daughter now.

4. Friar Laurence (IV, i) to Juliet about her marriage to Paris:

ಶ

I hear thou must, and nothing may <u>prorogue</u> it,
On Thursday next be married to this county.

ಶ

5. Juliet (IV, i) contemplating taking the potion:

ಶ

Where bloody Tybalt yet but green in earth
Lies festering in his shroud, where as they say
At some hours in the night spirits <u>resort</u>. . .

ಶ

6. Friar Laurence (IV, i) to Juliet:

ಶ

The roses in thy lips and cheeks shall fade
To <u>waned</u> ashes. . .

ಶ

7. Lord Capulet (IV, ii) to his servant:

ಶ

Sirrah, go hire me twenty <u>cunning</u> cooks.

ಶ

© 1993 by The Center for Applied Research in Education

8.   Juliet (IV, ii) to her father:

ʚ

> *To you and your behests, and am enjoined*
> *By holy Laurence to fall <u>prostrate</u> here,*
> *And beg your pardon.*

ʚ

9.   Juliet (IV, iii) responding to her mother's request for help:

ʚ

> *No madam, we have <u>culled</u> such necessaries*
> *As are behoveful for our state tomorrow.*

ʚ

10.   Juliet (IV, iii) contemplating taking the potion:

ʚ

> *Shall I not then be <u>stifled</u> in the vault,*
> *To whose foul mouth no healthsome air breathes in. . .*

ʚ

Vocabulary Review Quiz
for
Romeo and Juliet
Act IV

Directions: For each of the italicized words in the sentences below, determine which letter best reflects the use of the word in this context. Place the letter corresponding to your answer in the space to the left of the item number.

____1. Juliet fears that the ghosts which some say *resort* at night in the family tomb will attack her.
In this context, *resort* means
A. run away from   B. go to frequently   C. rest   D. live

____2. Juliet's family mistakes, her *pensive* behavior for grief over Tybalt's death.
In this context, *pensive* means
A. joyful and happy   B. lonesome   C. reflective and sad
D. sleepy and tearful

____3. Juliet wept *immoderately* for Romeo's banishment.
In this context, *immoderately* means
A. excessively   B. sufficiently   C. indecently   D. immorally

____4. Begging forgiveness, Juliet *prostrates* herself to her father.
In this context, *prostrates* means
A. falls before   B. hurls   C. bares   D. scolds

____5. Tybalt is known to be a *cunning* swordsman.
In this context, *cunning* means
A. famous   B. smiling   C. terrible   D. skillful

____6. Juliet *entreats* her father not to make her marry Paris.
In this context, *entreats* means
A. cries   B. begs   C. asks   D. denies

____7. Romeo and Benvolio *culled* Rosaline's name from the Capulets' guest list.
In this context, *culled* means
A. selected   B. took   C. heard   D. read

_____8. Juliet feared she would *stifle* in the tomb.
In this context, *stifle* means

A. give up hope   B. become insane   C. thrive   D. smother

_____9. Juliet tries to *prorogue* her marriage to Paris but fails.
In this context, *prorogue* means

A. annul   B. dissolve   C. postpone   D. hasten

_____10. After Juliet took the potion, the color *waned* from her cheeks.
In this context, *waned* means

A. decreased in intensity   B. became greater   C. became less full
D. flushed

ACT V

© 1993 by The Center for Applied Research in Education

NAME:_____   DATE:_____

Focusing Activities
for
Romeo and Juliet
Scenarios for Improvisation
Act V

Directions: Presented below are locations and situations involving characters. Before reading an individual scene, pretend to be one of the characters and act out the situation. Don't worry about speaking like characters in Shakespeare's play; just try to imagine how you would react to the situation and use your own language. Take a few minutes to discuss with the other performers what you would like to do. Be prepared to act out your scene for others in the class. Afterward, classmates outside your group may discuss what they've seen.

scene i.   *Scene:* Romeo's quarters in Mantua.

Characters: Romeo and Balthasar.

Situation: Balthasar brings Romeo news of Juliet. What does he tell Romeo and what does Romeo propose to do?

scene iii.   *Scene:* Outside the Capulet family tomb.

Characters: The Prince, Friar Laurence, Lord and Lady Capulet, Lord Montague.

Situation: Romeo and Juliet are dead and the Prince's guards have found Friar Laurence nearby. Friar Laurence offers an explanation. How do the Prince, Lord and Lady Capulet, and Lord Montague react?

Focusing Activities
for
Romeo and Juliet
Small Group Discussion Questions
Act V

Directions: Before reading scenes in Act V, discuss the questions in small groups. You may wish to make notes about your discussion, so you can share them with classmates or refer back to them after you've read the scene.

scene i. How do you think Romeo will react when he learns that Juliet is dead?

scenes ii and iii. What problems do you think may keep Friar Laurence's plan for Romeo and Juliet to be together from succeeding?

© 1993 by The Center for Applied Research in Education

NAME:_____   DATE:_____

Focusing Activities
for
Romeo and Juliet
Speculation Journal
Act V

Directions: This activity will help you become involved actively with reading the play by helping you to determine a definite purpose for reading. Before you read these scenes in Act V, take a few minutes to respond in writing to the questions below. Don't worry about correct answers here. Use your own experience or what you have read in the play to speculate about what you think might happen. After reading a scene you may find that characters reacted differently than you thought. Don't worry about these differences; just make note of them because you will have opportunities to share these differences in other activities.

scene i. What do you think Romeo will do once he learns of Juliet's "death"?

scene ii. What problems do you see that may spoil Friar Laurence's plan for Romeo and Juliet to be together?

scene iii. From the Prologue to the play in Act I, we know that Romeo and Juliet will die. If you were the Prince, what punishment would you impose upon Lords Capulet and Montague for the lovers' deaths?

After Reading the Play: Now that you have finished reading the play, which of your speculations were most accurate? How do you account for them? Which ones were least like the action of the play? Why do you think you speculated as you did?

157

Prereading Activity
for
Romeo and Juliet
Vocabulary
Act V

Directions: Shakespeare uses the following words in Act V. The section below provides a brief definition of each word and provides a sentence to illustrate its meaning.

Definitions.

scene i

1. **kindred:** (n.) persons related to each other; family, tribe.
   Example: My *kindred* gathered for an annual reunion at Grandma's house.

2. **loath-
   some:** (adj.) revolting, disgusting, repulsive.
   Example: The way that David played with his food in the junior high cafeteria was *loathsome*.

3. **presage:** (v.) to foreshadow; to forecast, predict.
   Example: Meteorologists often fail when they try to *presage* the exact path of a storm system.

4. **straight:** (adv.) soon, immediately, directly.
   Example: The children came *straight* home after school.

scene ii

5. **associate:** (v.) to connect or bring into relation; to join as a companion or ally.
   Example: Jim *associated* himself with the environmental movement by starting a recycling program.

6. **pestilence:** (n.) a deadly epidemic disease.
   Example: The bubonic plague spread *pestilence* throughout medieval Europe.

scene iii

7. **adventure:** (v.) to take a chance or risk; to dare.
   Example: Jamie *adventured* to climb the tree.

8. **aloof:**   (adv.) reserved or indifferent.
   Example: The cat remained *aloof* from the commotion of the party preparations.

9. **haughty:**   (adj.) proud, snobbish, arrogant.
   Example: We expected Denise to be *haughty* after winning the contest, but she wasn't.

10. **restorative:**   (n.) a means of restoring a person to consciousness; a means of renewing or revitalizing something.
    Example: We used the smelling salts as a *restorative* after Herman fainted.

Prereading Activity
for
Romeo and Juliet
Plot Summaries
Act V

Directions: To help you better understand and follow Shakespeare's play, read the summary of specific scenes immediately before you begin to read the original. If you get lost during the scene, refer to the summary again.

Act V,
scene i

In Mantua, Romeo reveals that he has had a strange dream. In the dream, Juliet has found him dead, kissed him, and he revives, becoming an emperor. Balthasar comes with the news that Juliet is dead, for Balthasar saw the burial. He tries to comfort Romeo with the idea that Juliet's soul is at peace and in heaven.

Romeo doesn't want to believe Juliet is dead. He asks for horses, so he can return to Verona to investigate for himself. He asks if Friar Laurence has sent a letter, but the servant has none.

Romeo swears to be with Juliet that night, and he remembers a druggist who is shady enough to sell him poison. Romeo buys a small bottle of poison from the druggist. Although the selling of poison is against the laws of the town, the druggist sells it because he needs the money. Romeo heads for Verona, where he plans to drink the poison beside Juliet's body.

Act V,
scene ii

Meanwhile, Friar John, whom Friar Laurence had sent to Mantua with a letter revealing the plan to Romeo, returns to Friar Laurence's cell. Friar John relates that he sought the help of another monk when he got to Mantua. But the other monk had been exposed to pestilence and, with Friar John, was isolated by the authorities. Having failed, Friar John returns to Verona with the letter. Friar Laurence realizes that Romeo will not be at the tomb when Juliet awakens, so he hurries to be there when she does and plans to hide Juliet in his cell until Romeo does come.

Act V,
scene iii

Thursday night, Paris and a page come to visit Juliet's grave. Paris tells the page to stand lookout and whistle if anyone approaches.

Romeo and Balthasar arrive. Romeo gives the servant a letter for Friar Laurence and then commands the servant not to interfere, regardless of what he may see or hear. Balthasar doesn't leave. Instead, he hides to see what Romeo will do.

Paris sees Romeo breaking into the tomb. Paris believes that Romeo has come to take revenge against the Capulets for being exiled. When Paris confronts Romeo, Romeo asks to be left alone. They fight and Romeo kills Paris. Romeo grants Paris's dying request to be placed beside Juliet.

When Romeo enters the tomb and sees Juliet's body, he recalls their love, takes the poison, and dies.

Friar Laurence, armed with tools to break into the tomb, arrives too late. He finds the bodies of Romeo and Paris. Hearing Juliet awaken, he goes to her and tries to get her out of the tomb. He tells her of the two deaths and offers to send her to a convent. Hearing the Prince's men on watch approaching, he exits.

Juliet realizes that Romeo has taken poison, but that his death was recent, for his lips are warm. Wanting to join him in death, Juliet tries to poison herself, first from the empty vial and then by kissing Romeo. It doesn't work, so she takes Romeo's dagger, stabs herself, and dies.

The watch comes and realizes that someone may still be around. Some of the guards go to get the Prince while others enter with Balthasar and another group with Friar Laurence.

When the Prince enters, he demands an explanation. Having heard the noise, Lord and Lady Capulet and later Lord Montague enter. All realize that Juliet has killed herself. Montague reveals that his wife has died from grief over Romeo's exile.

Friar Laurence then explains the secret marriage, the banishment, and his plan to have Juliet only seem dead so she could be reunited with Romeo. He also explains why the plan didn't work. Both Balthasar's testimony and Romeo's letter demonstrate the truth of the friar's story. As the sun is about to dawn, the Prince points out the consequences of the feud to both Capulet and Montague and that no further punishment is necessary. The two men put aside the feud and promise to raise a statue to Romeo and Juliet to remind the town of the children's fate.

Class Period:

CHARACTER ASSIGNMENTS FOR ORAL READING GROUPS

Romeo and Juliet

Session 8: Act V, scenes i, ii, iii

Characters	*Group 1*	*Group 2*	*Group 3*	*Group 4*
Romeo	___	___	___	___
Balthasar, Lord Capulet	___	___	___	___
Apothecary, Watchman	___	___	___	___
Friar John, Prince	___	___	___	___
Friar Laurence	___	___	___	___
Paris, Lord Montague	___	___	___	___
Page, Boy	___	___	___	___
Juliet	___	___	___	___

162

During-Reading Activity
for
Romeo and Juliet
Character Diary 5
Act V
Thursday through Friday Dawn

Directions: Use the space below to record your character's reactions to the events that occur in Act V of *Romeo and Juliet*. Remember to include a summary of events, explain how your character learned of them, and give your character's reactions to these events.

The Personal Diary of

_____
(character's name)

Thursday, July 24, 1597 (Act V, scenes i and ii)
Night

_____

_____

_____

_____

_____

_____

Friday, July 25, 1597 (Act V, scene iii)
Morning

_____

_____

_____

_____

_____

_____

_____

During-Reading Activity
for
Romeo and Juliet
Guide to Character Development: Romeo
Act V

Shakespeare reveals his characters in four ways:

- through what the characters say to other characters in dialogue;

- through what the characters reveal about their thoughts through long speeches to the audience called *soliloquies*;

- through what other characters say about them;

- through what they do, their actions.

As you read the play, examine the following scenes for what they reveal about Romeo's character and fill in the chart briefly using your own words. If you need more room, use the back of the page.

Scene	What Romeo says, does, or what others say about him	What this reveals about Romeo's character
Act V, scene i Romeo learns of Juliet's "death."		
Act V, scene iii Romeo goes to Juliet's tomb		

© 1993 by The Center for Applied Research in Education

NAME:_____   DATE:_____

During-Reading Activity
for
Romeo and Juliet
Guide to Character Development: Juliet
Act V

Shakespeare reveals his characters in four ways:

* through what the characters say to other characters in dialogue;

* through what the characters reveal about their thoughts through long speeches to the audience called *soliloquies*;

* through what other characters say about them;

* through what they do, their actions.

As you read the play, examine the following scene for what it reveals about Juliet's character and fill in the chart briefly using your own words. If you need more room, use the back of the page.

Scene	What Juliet says, does, or what others say about her	What this reveals about Juliet's character
Act V, scene iii Juliet awakens in the tomb		

NAME:_____   DATE:_____

Postreading Activity
for
Romeo and Juliet
Comprehension Check
Act V

Directions: After you've read all of Act V, use the following questions to check how well you've understood what you've read. For each question, select the most appropriate answer from the choices listed below it. Place the letter corresponding to your answer in the space to the left of the item number.

_____1. After Balthasar tells Romeo of Juliet's death, what does Romeo do?

A. He buys a new dagger to kill himself.
B. He purchases a new horse.
C. He stabs himself immediately.
D. He buys poison.
E. He goes looking for Friar Laurence.

_____2. According to the play, what prevents Brother John from delivering Friar Laurence's letter to Romeo?

A. He can't find Romeo.
B. He's put under quarantine.
C. He loses the letter.
D. Romeo rides past him on the road.
E. He gives it to Balthasar.

_____3. Why does Paris think that Romeo has come to Juliet's tomb?

A. To take revenge for being exiled.
B. To see Juliet.
C. To kill Paris.
D. To kill Friar Laurence.
E. To kill himself.

_____4. What does Juliet mean when she realizes that Romeo has drunk poison and says,

ﻉﻤ

O Churl! drunk all, and left no friendly drop
To help me after?

ﻉﻤ

A. Romeo suffered a terrible death.
B. That Romeo took all the poison and left her none.
C. That she will die more easily than he will.
D. That she will have to continue to live.
E. That she will enter a convent.

_____5. At the end of the play, the Prince declines to punish either Capulet or Montague. What have Capulet and Montague learned from the deaths of Romeo and Juliet?

A. That each blames the other.
B. That everything was Friar Laurence's fault.
C. That the deaths were no one's fault.
D. That the Prince should pardon everyone.
E. That their quarrel was foolish.

Postreading Activity
for
Romeo and Juliet
Small Group Discussion to Check Comprehension
Act V

Directions: After you've read all of Act V, in small groups, discuss each of the
following questions briefly. Use the space below each question to note
points you may want to share later. If you need more room, use the
back of the page.

1. After Balthasar tells Romeo of Juliet's death, what does Romeo prepare
    to do?

2. What prevents Brother John from delivering Friar Laurence's letter
    to Romeo?

3. Why does Paris think that Romeo has come to Juliet's tomb?

4. What does Juliet mean when she realizes that Romeo has drunk poison
    and says,

    ❧

    O Churl! drunk all, and left no friendly drop
    To help me after?

    ❧

5. At the end of the play, the Prince declines to punish either Capulet or Montague. What have Capulet and Montague learned from the deaths of Romeo and Juliet?

Postreading Activity
for
Romeo and Juliet
Critical Thinking Questions
Act V

Directions: To help develop your understanding of Act V, take time to think about and discuss these questions. The first question is the focus question and the point of the discussion. Don't be concerned that you may not be able to answer it at first. Proceed to the exploration questions and then return to the focus question.

Focus Question. For what reasons would you or members of society hold Romeo and Juliet responsible for their own deaths? Who else might you hold responsible and how would you punish them?

Exploration Questions.

1. What events occur in the play, which Friar Laurence hadn't expected, that help bring about the unhappy ending?

2. What types of events do the mass media (newspapers, magazines, radio, and television) call tragic?

3. What decisions have you made impulsively that you later regretted?

4. Under what circumstances would you, like the apothecary, go against the law to make money?

5. Why might we view Romeo and Juliet's suicides today more as impulsive acts than tragic ones?

6. In what ways might the arguments that you would use to talk Romeo and Juliet out of suicide differ from the ones that adults would use?

Postreading Activity
for
Romeo and Juliet
Language Exploration:
Apostrophe
Act V

You're walking down the hallway after school and you pass a classmate. You turn and call out, "Kim, could I speak to you?" Kim doesn't hear you and continues on her way. You mutter, "That's O.K., Kim, it wasn't very important anyway."

In the first line of dialogue, you addressed Kim directly. In the second, although Kim was no longer within hearing, you pretended she was present and aired your feelings.

Poets also use the device of having a character speak to a person or an abstract idea even though the person or idea isn't or can't be present. This particular device is called *apostrophe*. Consider the following examples:

❧

Death, be not proud.

❧

Rose, where'd you get that red?

❧

Twinkle, twinkle little star,
How I wonder what you are.

❧

In the first example, the speaker addresses Death and tells it not to be proud. This suggests that the speaker doesn't fear death. The second example allows the speaker to address a flower and speculate how it came to be red. The nursery rhyme in the third example lets the speaker address a star and contemplate it.

Directions: The following passages from Acts I–V are examples of apostrophe. Working in pairs, small groups, or as your teacher directs, review each passage in the context of the play and decide what the apostrophe suggests about the speaker's attitude towards the absent person.

1.   Mercutio (Act II, scene i):

ॐ

Romeo! humors! madman! passion! lover!
Appear thou in the likeness of a sign;
Speak but one rhyme and I am satisfied

ॐ

2.   Romeo (Act II, scene ii):

ॐ

She speaks.
O, speak again, bright angel!

ॐ

3.   Juliet (Act II, scene ii):

ॐ

O Romeo, Romeo! wherefore art thou Romeo?
Deny thy father and refuse thy name.

ॐ

4.   Romeo (Act III, scene i) after Tybalt kills Mercutio:

ॐ

O sweet Juliet,
Thy beauty hath made me effeminate
And in my temper sof'ned valor's steel!

ॐ

© 1993 by The Center for Applied Research in Education

5. Nurse (Act III, scene iii):

᪥

O Tybalt, Tybalt, the best friend I had!
O courteous Tybalt! honest gentleman!

᪥

6. Juliet (Act III, scene iii):

᪥

Oh, my poor lord, what tongue shall smooth thy name
When I, thy three-hours wife have mangled it?

᪥

7. Juliet (Act III, scene v):

᪥

O Fortune, Fortune! all men call thee fickle.

᪥

8. Capulet (Act IV, scene v):

᪥

O child, O child! my soul and not my child!
Dead art thou

᪥

9.   Romeo (Act V, scene i)

≥≥

Then I defy you, stars!

≥≥

10.   Romeo (Act V, scene ii):

≥≥

Well, Juliet, I will lie with thee tonight.

≥≥

NAME:_____   DATE:_____

Postreading Activity
for
Romeo and Juliet
Language Exploration Review Quiz

Directions: Now that you've discussed all Language Exploration Activities, use the following questions to check how well you can apply what you have learned to new selections. For each question, select the most appropriate answer from the choices listed below it. Place the letter corresponding to your answer in the space to the left of the item number.

_____ 1. Lord Capulet (Act I, scene ii) comments to Paris about Juliet,

ଧ

Earth hath swallowed all my hopes but she:

ଧ

The image suggests
A. Paris can marry Juliet.
B. There's been a landslide.
C. Paris cannot marry Juliet.
D. All Capulet's other children are dead and buried.
E. Capulet has no hope of seeing Juliet married.

_____ 2. "Earth has swallowed all my hopes" is an example of

A. Changed sentence order
B. Simile
C. Metaphor
D. Personification
E. Apostrophe

_____ 3. Lady Capulet (Act I, scene iii) praises Paris to Juliet,

ଧ

Verona's summer hath not such a flower.

ଧ

Lady Capulet suggests that
A. Paris is handsome.
B. Paris is a sissy.
C. Paris is more attractive than any flower in Verona.
D. Paris is ugly.
E. Paris is a good catch.

175

_____4. "Verona's summer hath not such a flower" is an example of
   A. Changed sentence order
   B. Simile
   C. Metaphor
   D. Personification
   E. Apostrophe

_____5. Mercutio (Act I, scene iv) states

ᘒ

I talk of dreams
Which are the children of an idle brain;

ᘒ

Mercutio suggests that
   A. Dreams come from lazy children.
   B. Dreams come from children.
   C. Dreams, like lazy children, come about as a result of having nothing to do.
   D. Dreams come from a brain that has nothing to do.
   E. Dreams are idle children.

_____6. Romeo (Act I, scene v) notices Juliet at the banquet and states

ᘒ

So shows a snowy dove trooping with crows
As yonder lady o'er her fellows shows.

ᘒ

Romeo suggests that
   A. Juliet stands out like a crow in a group of white doves.
   B. Juliet is beautiful.
   C. Juliet's hair is as dark as a crow's feathers.
   D. Juliet's beauty makes her stand out like a dove in a flock of crows.
   E. Juliet's beauty makes her stand out from all the other beautiful girls at the banquet.

_____7. "So shows a snowy dove trooping with crows/As yonder lady o'er her fellows shows" is an example of
   A. Changed sentence order
   B. Simile
   C. Metaphor
   D. Personification
   E. Apostrophe

____8.   "Here comes the furious Tybalt back again" is an example of

   A. Changed sentence order
   B. Simile
   C. Metaphor
   D. Personification
   E. Apostrophe

____9.   Before taking Friar Laurence's potion, Juliet speculates what may happen to her in the family tomb,

ᵴ

   And, in this rage, with some great kinsman's bone
   As with a club dash out desp'rate brains.

ᵴ

Juliet suggests here that she may
   A. Use a bone from a dead ancestor to club herself to death.
   B. Go mad in the tomb.
   C. Break down the door of the tomb with a bone.
   D. Beat on the door of the tomb with a bone.
   E. Be killed by the ghost of her ancestors.

____10.   Once beside Juliet's body, Romeo states

ᵴ

   Oh true Apothecary!
   Thy drugs are quick.

ᵴ

In these lines, Romeo lets the audience know that
   A. The Apothecary is coming.
   B. The Apothecary lied about the poison.
   C. The Apothecary didn't trick Romeo.
   D. The poison is strong and works quickly.
   E. The Apothecary will be punished.

NAME: _____   DATE: _____

Postreading Activity
for
Romeo and Juliet
Vocabulary in Context
Act V

Directions: In each of the passages below you will find one of the words from the prereading vocabulary list for Act V. Review the definitions given in the prereading vocabulary. Working individually, in pairs, or in small groups as your teacher directs, examine each of the underlined words in the following passages from Act V. For each word, use the appropriate meaning and develop a brief interpretation of the passage within the context of the play.

1. Balthasar (V, i) to Romeo:

    I saw her laid low in her <u>kindred's</u> vault. . .

2. Romeo (V, i) to the Apothecary:

    There is thy gold, worse poison to men's souls,
    Doing ore murder in this <u>loathsome</u> world. . .

3. Romeo (V, i) commenting on his dream:

    My dreams <u>presage</u> some joyful news at hand.

© 1993 by The Center for Applied Research in Education© 1993 by The Center for Applied Research in Education

4.   Romeo to Balthsar (V, i)

&

Get thee gone.
And hire some horses; I'll be with thee <u>straight</u>.

&

5.   Friar John (V, ii) to Friar Laurence:

&

Going to find a barefoot brother out,
One of our order, to <u>associate</u> me,
Here in this city. . .

&

6.   Friar John (V, ii) to Friar Laurence

&

Suspecting that we both were in a house
Where infectious <u>pestilence</u> did reign. . .

&

7.   Page (V, iii) after Paris orders him to go away:

&

I am almost afraid to stand alone,
Here in the churchyard, yet I will <u>adventure</u>.

&

179

8.   Romeo (V, iii) to Balthasar:

ﭜ

Upon thy life I charge thee,
Whate'er thou hearest or seest, stand all <u>aloof</u>,
And do not interrupt me in my course.

ﭜ

9.   Paris (V, iii) seeing Romeo at Juliet's tomb:

ﭜ

This is that <u>haughty</u> Montague,
That murdered my love's cousin. . .

ﭜ

10.   Juliet (V, iii) to the dead Romeo:

ﭜ

I will kiss thy lips,
Haply some poison yet doth hang on them,
To make me die with a <u>restorative</u>.

ﭜ

NAME:_____   DATE:_____

Vocabulary Review Quiz
for
Romeo and Juliet
Act V

Directions: For each of the italicized words in the sentences below, determine which letter best reflects the use of the word in this context. Place the letter corresponding to your answer in the space to the left of the item number.

_____1. Rosaline remains *aloof* from Romeo at the Capulets' party.
In this context, *aloof* means

A. angry   B. concerned for   C. indifferent   D. enthusiastic

_____2. Friar John is not allowed to search for Romeo because officials fear the friar has been exposed to *pestilence*.
In this context, *pestilence* means

A. epidemic disease   B. excessive dirt   C. knowledge   D. salvation

_____3. Friar John seeks to *associate* himself with a member of his order.
In this context, *associate* means

A. identify with   B. join as a companion   C. meet
D. communicate with

_____4. Hearing that Juliet has died, Romeo sees the entire world as *loathsome*.
In this context, *loathsome* means

A. unhealthy   B. repulsive   C. sad   D. degrading

_____5. Juliet was buried with her *kindred*.
In this context, *kindred* means

A. casket   B. family   C. enemies   D. goodness

_____6. In fairy tales, a kiss is often a *restorative* for a spell.
In this context, *restorative* means

A. a way of discovering   B. a way of increasing
C. a way of revitalizing   D. a way of hiding

_____7. Romeo rode *straight* to Juliet's tomb.
In this context, *straight* means

A. quickly   B. sadly   C. swiftly   D. directly

181

_____8. Romeo believes that his dreams *presage* the future.
In this context, *presage* means
A. retell   B. foretell   C. obscure   D. defer

_____9. Tybalt is *haughty* when he challenges Romeo to fight.
In this context, *haughty* means
A. angry   B. arrogant   C. curious   D. handsome

_____10. Juliet *adventures* to take the potion that Friar Laurence gave her.
In this context, *adventures* means
A. dares   B. fears   C. desires   D. refuses

EXTENDING ACTIVITIES

Overview of
Extending Activities
for
Romeo and Juliet

Directions: Now that you've completed your formal study of *Romeo and Juliet*, the extending activities listed below will provide you with opportunities to extend your understanding of the play. Remember that these are suggestions of things you might do. Perhaps you will think of others or your teacher may have additional suggestions. Your teacher can provide you with specific sets of directions for *acting out, oral interpretation, puppet theater, masks, writing assignments,* and *visual displays.*

Acting Out

1. Dramatize a missing scene related to the characters and situations in the play. For example, how does the apothecary explain selling the poison to his wife?

2. Present a scene from the play in a modern context. Use contemporary settings, words, and ideas.

Oral Interpretation

Present a prepared reading of the speech of a single character, between two characters, or of an entire scene. Keep in mind that oral interpretation involves communicating the words effectively *without* actually memorizing a script and acting out the scene with full costumes and props.

Puppetry and Masks

1. Make paper bag puppets and present a scene from the play.

2. Create paper plate masks for specific characters and present a scene from the play wearing them.

Writing Assignments

1. Write an alternative ending to the play.

2. Research some element of life in the time of Romeo and Juliet (Italy during between 1500–1600 A.D.).

3. Pretending to be one of the characters in the play, create a letter or note to another character.

Visual Displays

1. Create a graffiti wall for Verona.

2. Create a time line for the play by listing the significant events in order.

3. Draw a comic strip or drawing for a scene from the play.

4. Create a filmstrip or video related to the play.

5. Construct a mobile using double-sided objects/characters from the play with a 3 × 5 card containing a description beneath each object.

6. Create a music video combining still pictures with music and words.

7. Select and depict 12 or 16 scenes from the play for a multiple panel quilt. Make each panel out of paper. For each panel of your quilt, create an illustration and write a caption that explains it. Create a border for each panel and tie or string them together to form a large wall hanging.

8. Research and build a Globe Theater model.

9. Research and present samples of Elizabethan cooking.

10. Research and present Elizabethan costumes.

11. Create a slide sound presentation on some aspect of the play.

© 1993 by The Center for Applied Research in Education

NAME:_____   DATE:_____

Extending Activities
for
Romeo and Juliet
Acting Out

Directions: From time to time during your study of *Romeo and Juliet*, you may have participated in an improvised scene from the play either before or after you read particular scenes. Now that you've read the entire play, here are some additional opportunities for you to act out and demonstrate your fuller understanding of the play and its characters. You may improvise these scenes or fully script and rehearse them.

1. Suppose you are the guidance counselor, Ms. Laurence. How do you suppose you would counsel Romeo about his problems in Act II, scene iii; Act II, scene vi; Act III, scene iii; or Act V, scene i?

2. Suppose you were the guidance counselor, Ms. Laurence. How would you counsel Juliet in Act I?

3. What would the apothecary, who sold the illegal poison to Romeo, say to his wife when he returned from being awakened?

4. It's after the party at the Capulets'. Tybalt is still angry about Romeo and his friends crashing the party. He calls the young men of the Capulet household together and convinces them to seek revenge. What does he say?

5. After the close of the play, Friar Laurence's abbot calls him in to explain his actions. What does he tell his superior?

6. Create a Heaven (or Hell) scene where all characters defend their lives or tell others what has happened in their lives.

7. Choose a scene and present it in modern context. For example, Leonard Bernstein used *Romeo and Juliet* as the basis for *West Side Story*. Instead of Verona, Italy, he set his version on New York City's West side. Instead of the party at the Capulets', he has Tony (Romeo) meet Maria (Juliet) at a high school dance.

8. Develop a segment for "60 Minutes," CBS (NBC or ABC) Evening News, "Entertainment Tonight," "Phil Donahue," "Oprah," "Geraldo," "Now It Can Be Told," or "A Current Affair" based upon *Romeo and Juliet*.

9. Create the "prequel" to *Romeo and Juliet* which explains how the feud between the Capulets and Montagues begins generations earlier.

10. Create a sequel to *Romeo and Juliet*.

Extending Activities
for
Romeo and Juliet
Oral Interpretation

Directions: Present a prepared reading of a speech or scene from *Romeo and Juliet*. Listed below are suggestions of solo and duet scenes to choose from. You may wish to check with your teacher and present other scenes.

To help you prepare your scene, work through all the steps.

Solo Scenes

Prince, Act I, sc. i—the Prince pronounces sentence upon the Houses of Capulet and Montague

Nurse, Act I, sc. iii—her recounting of Juliet as a child

Mercutio, Act I, sc. iv—"Queen Mab Speech"

Juliet Act IV, sc. iii—the soliloquy before Juliet takes the potion

Romeo, Act V, sc. iii—the soliloquy from Paris' death until his own

Duet Scenes

Romeo and Benvolio, Act I, sc. i—the discussion of Rosaline

Tybalt and Lord Capulet, Act I, sc. i—their argument over Romeo crashing the party

Romeo and Juliet, Act I, sc. v—their first meeting

Romeo and Juliet, Act II, sc. ii—the first balcony scene

Friar Laurence and Romeo, Act II, sc. iii—Romeo's discussion of wedding plans

Juliet and Nurse, Act II, sc. v—the Nurse's telling Juliet of the wedding plans

Juliet and Nurse, Act III, sc. ii—Nurse's informing Juliet of Tybalt's death and Romeo's banishment

Romeo and Juliet, Act III, sc. v—the second balcony scene where Romeo and Juliet part

Juliet and Lady Capulet, Act III, sc. v—Lady Capulet's informing Juliet that she is to marry Paris

Romeo and Apothecary, Act V, sc. i—Romeo's buying the poison

Friar Laurence and Juliet, Act V, sc. iii—the Friar's rescuing of Juliet from the tomb

© 1993 by The Center for Applied Research in Education

*Steps for
Preparing an
Oral Interpretation*

1. Select a scene or passage that you really like. The passage should have a definite beginning, high point, and an end. Remember that you will be doing a prepared reading and not memorizing a script. Most often oral interpreters either stand before their audience or sit on a stool.

2. Prepare a script to work from. You may wish to type out the selection or reproduce it from a book. You'll need a copy that you can make notes on. Mount your script on black construction paper, so you can read from it easily without having to hold it with both hands. Keep the pages of your manuscript loose, so you can either slide them out of the way or shift them under each other as you finish reading them.

3. Analyze the script. As you work through the analysis, make notes to yourself in pencil on your script.

   a. Read the whole passage and decide what it's about. Because you've already read the whole play, you know where your selection fits into the development of the characters.

   b. Read the whole piece several times and decide what the overall effect of the piece is.

   c. Make notes of things you don't understand—allusions, words, and so forth. Check the footnotes in your text or look up unfamiliar words in the dictionary. Remember that the meaning of particular words may have changed since Shakespeare's time. If you have a problem understanding a particular word, check the glossary of terms found in most *Complete Works of Shakespeare* in your library.

   d. As you look at individual words, you should know how to pronounce all of them as well as know both their denotative meaning (the dictionary meaning) and their connotative meaning (the emotional subtleties that come from using the word in a particular context).

   e. Where does the scene take place? Is it a public place, like the streets of Verona, or a private one, like Juliet's chamber? Who speaks here and what is the speaker's emotional state at the time? What has happened before this scene?

   f. Examine the overall organization of the scene. What emotions do the characters reveal in this scene? What changes in character, motivation, or emotions occur during the scene? For example, in Juliet's soliloquy in Act IV, iii, Juliet considers three or four consequences to taking the potion. Decide how you can convey these changes with your voice.

4. Begin practicing aloud. Read the passage out loud, working either with a partner or with a tape recorder. Listen to yourself. Experiment with different readings. Underline words you wish to emphasize. Make marginal notes about the emotions you wish to portray in different parts.

5. Write a brief introduction to your scene, setting it up for your listeners. The following example could be used to introduce Act II, scene v:

   The day after Romeo and Juliet have met and fallen in love, Juliet sends the Nurse to meet Romeo to learn about the plans he's made for them to marry. She has sent the Nurse at nine in the morning, expecting her to return within a half hour. It's now noon and Juliet waits anxiously in her parents' garden.

6. Once you've decided on how you wish to read your selection, practice, practice, practice! Your goal in these sessions is not to memorize the words but to learn the interpretation, so that when you present it, you can concentrate on a smooth performance.

7. Perform the piece. Some interpreters prefer to stand while others prefer to sit upon stools. You may hold the script in your hands or use a music stand or lectern.

Extending Activities
for
Romeo and Juliet
Puppet Theater

One way to present scenes from *Romeo and Juliet* without having to worry about elaborate sets or costumes is to use puppets made from brown paper bags. You can make your own puppets using construction paper, scissors, rubber cement, crayons, and felt-tip markers. You can use a table turned sideways as a stage for the puppeteers to hide behind. If you feel that you need scenery, make a mural and use masking tape to secure it to the wall behind you.

Steps to Making and Performing Scene with Puppets

1. Select a scene that you want to perform. Listed below are scenes for two, three, or more actors.

Scenes for Two Actors

Romeo and Benvolio, Act I, sc. i—their discussion of Rosaline

Tybalt and Lord Capulet, Act I, sc. i—their argument over Romeo crashing the party

Romeo and Juliet, Act I, sc. v—their first meeting

Romeo and Juliet, Act II, sc. ii—first balcony scene

Friar Laurence and Romeo, Act II, sc. iii—their discussion of love and wedding plans

Juliet and Nurse, Act II, sc. v—Nurse's telling Juliet of the wedding plans

Juliet and Nurse, Act III, sc. ii—Nurse's telling Juliet of Tybalt's death and Romeo's banishment

Romeo and Juliet, Act III, sc. v—second balcony scene where Romeo and Juliet part

Juliet and Lady Capulet, Act III, sc. v—Lady Capulet's informing Juliet that she is to marry Paris

Romeo and Apothecary, Act V, sc. i—Romeo buying the poison

Friar Laurence and Juliet, Act V, sc. iii—Friar coming to rescue Juliet from the tomb

Scenes for Three or More Actors

Romeo, Benvolio, and Capulet's servant, Act I, sc. ii—Romeo reading the guest list for the servant who can't read

Juliet, Lady Capulet, and Nurse, Act I, sc. iii—Lady Capulet asking Juliet how she feels about getting married

Romeo, Mercutio, and Nurse, Act II, sc. iv—Mercutio insulting the Nurse before she learns of Romeo's plans

Juliet, Lady Capulet, Lord Capulet, Nurse, Act III, sc. v—Lady and Lord Capulet telling Juliet that she will marry Paris

Juliet, Paris, Friar Laurence, Act IV, sc. i—Paris and Juliet's meeting at the cell of Friar Laurence

2. Design and make puppets. In making your puppets, refer to **Figure 1.** To make your puppet talk, insert your hand into the bag and curl your fingers so the upper face on the top of the bag moves up and down.

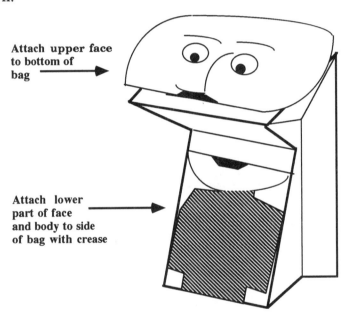

Attach upper face to bottom of bag

Attach lower part of face and body to side of bag with crease

Figure 1
Paper Bag Puppet

3. Prepare your script as if you were doing an oral interpretation. *See* specific directions entitled "Extending Activity for *Romeo and Juliet:* Oral Interpretation."

4. Decide how you can make your puppet appear to walk and move.

5. Practice, practice, practice.

Extending Activity
for
Romeo and Juliet
Paper Plate Masks

Directions: One way to help you present scenes from *Romeo and Juliet* is to create a half mask to represent the character in a specific scene. When you present your scene, hold the mask in front of you to create the character.

To make your own mask, you will need:

large white paper plates (do not use plastic plates)

large craft stick

scissors

glue (either rubber cement or hot melt glue gun work well)

assorted construction paper, ribbon, cloth, cardboard, yarn to make hair, hats and other decorations that help represent the character

crayons, colored pencils, or felt-tip markers

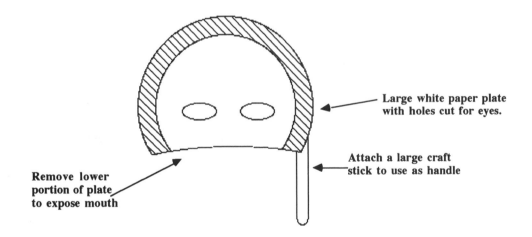

Figure 2
Paper Plate Mask

Extending Activities
for
Romeo and Juliet
Writing Assignments

Directions: Given below are some ideas for possible writing assignments based on your understanding of the characters and situations in *Romeo and Juliet*.

1. You are the casting director for a new film version of *Romeo and Juliet*. Write a letter to the film's producers explaining who from among current film, television, or rock and roll stars you would like to cast in each of the play's principal roles: Romeo, Juliet, Benvolio, Mercutio, Lord Capulet, Lady Capulet, the Nurse, Paris, the Prince, Friar Laurence.

2. Write new lyrics to a popular song and create a new love theme for *Romeo and Juliet*.

3. Write a new or more satisfying ending to the play.

4. Create a "meeting of minds" where characters from *Romeo and Juliet* interact with characters from other literature. You may also want to have the characters interact with their authors.

5. Create a children's version of the play. Check *Shake Hands with Shakespeare* or Charles and Caroline Lamb's *Tales from Shakespeare*.

6. Create an illustrated children's book based upon *Romeo and Juliet*.

7. Imagine that before Juliet takes the potion, she writes a note to her parents. What does she say as she prepares to feign her own death and join Romeo in exile?

8. Investigate the Globe Theater restoration project in London and report your findings to the class.

9. Research the food, clothing, housing, festivals or celebrations for either Elizabethan England or 16th-century Italy and present your findings.

10. Using the character diary that you kept during your reading of the play, write a letter to your cousin in Venice, another Italian city-state, relaying both the events of the previous week and your response to them.

11. Early in the play, Romeo tells Friar Laurence that he has fallen in love with Rosaline, but he is out of favor with her. Write a note from Romeo and an answer from Rosaline.

12. As one of the characters in the play, write a letter to either "Dear Abby" or "Ann Landers" and imagine the columnist's reply.

13. Research the development and historical aspect of weapons used in the play or in Shakespeare's time.

PART THREE

Appendices

Appendix A

EVALUATING READING PROCESS ACTIVITIES

This section will show you how to evaluate and assign grades for reading process activities for a *Romeo and Juliet* unit and how to set up and review reading activity folders.

It also reviews the instructional goals for all activities and suggests specific guidelines for evaluating them.

ASSESSING STUDENTS' PARTICIPATION

With a reading workshop approach to literature, just as with a writing workshop approach to written composition, you must decide how to assess students' participation in process activities and to evaluate the formal products that demonstrate learning as well. The activities in this resource provide opportunities for students to improve their reading, writing, speaking, listening, and critical thinking processes as well as learn about *Romeo and Juliet*. Although you don't need to grade all the process activities formally, you will want to review and respond to your students' work as they read the play. If you and your students were to devote three weeks to a unit on *Romeo and Juliet*, you might use the percentages listed in the table below.

SUGGESTED COMPONENTS OF UNIT GRADE

Activity	Percentage of Unit Grade	Numbers of Items and Point Values	Total
Prereading activities	8%	(8 reading sessions @ 5 pts.)	40 pts.
Response journal or character diaries	25%	(5 [one per act] @ 25 pts.)	125 pts.
Postreading activities	10%	(5 summary sessions @ 10 pts.)	50 pts.
Comprehension checks	10%	(5 @ 10 pts.)	50 pts.
Vocabulary review quizzes	10%	(5 @ 10 pts.)	50 pts.
Language exploration activities	10%	(5 @ 10 pts.)	50 pts.
Language exploration review quiz	2%		10 pts.
Individual or group extending activity	25%		125 pts.
Total	**100%**		**500 pts.**

SETTING UP AND REVIEWING READING ACTIVITY FOLDERS

Reading folders allow the students to keep their prereading, during-reading, and postreading activities together for the entire unit. Any type of folder works well although two pocket folders allow storage of response journals or character diaries on one side and other reading process activities on the other.

To monitor students' progress and to provide formative evaluation, review approximately 20 percent of the students' folders for each class period at the end of each day. Select the folders at random, so the class doesn't know when you will check any individual's work. Take a few minutes to skim and scan the work in each folder.

As you review each student's work, check to see that the student understands the directions and purpose of each activity. Use brief comments to praise the work specifically and to point out specific deficiencies. Then record the date of your review and any point values. You might try using +√ for outstanding work, √ for satisfactory work, and -√ for less than satisfactory work because students may find these symbols less threatening than traditional letter grades. You can translate codes like these into a numerical equivalent for your records: for example, awarding 5 points for outstanding work, 4 for satisfactory, and 3 for less than satisfactory.

INSTRUCTIONAL GOALS AND EVALUATIVE GUIDELINES FOR SPECIFIC READING ACTIVITIES

This section provides the instructional goals for specific reading process activities and suggests possible ways to assess them.

Focusing Activities

Although students complete only *one* focusing activity for a particular scene, all focusing activities share two common *instructional goals*:

🍃 to help students use prior knowledge related to *Romeo and Juliet*

🍃 to establish a purpose for reading a scene

Scenarios for Improvisation

Guidelines for Assessment:

Does the student

🍃 participate actively as either actor or audience?

🍃 provide logical motivations for the character's actions?

🍃 establish actions that are consistent with setting and existing information about character?

Prereading Discussion Questions

Guidelines for Assessment:

Does the student

🍃 participate in discussion?

🍃 share ideas willingly?

- ❧ allow others to share ideas?

- ❧ provide explanation or support for ideas?

- ❧ provide speculations that are consistent with the student's existing knowledge of *Romeo and Juliet*?

Speculation Journal

Guidelines for Assessment:

Does the student

- ❧ address the issues contained in the question(s)?

- ❧ provide explanation or support for ideas?

- ❧ provide speculations that are consistent with the student's existing knowledge of *Romeo and Juliet*?

Introducing the Play With Videotape

Guidelines for Assessment:

Does the student

- ❧ attempt to answer all the questions?

- ❧ address the issues in the prompt?

- ❧ have an overall understanding of the scene and its conflict?

Vocabulary

Instructional Goals:

- ❧ to review definitions of less familiar words

- ❧ to demonstrate the effect of context upon meaning

Plot Summaries

Instructional Goals:

- ❧ to establish an overview of each scene

- ❧ to provide a reference for the student when Shakespeare's text seems incomprehensible

Response Journals

As one of two on-going writing-to-learn activities that students may use during their reading of *Romeo and Juliet*, the response journal has two *instructional goals*:

- ❧ to summarize and reflect upon the meaning of the play

❧ to recognize, record, and comment upon repeated elements found in the play, such as symbols, motifs, themes, character development, or figurative language

Guidelines for Assessment:

Does the student

- ❧ record an entry for each reading session?
- ❧ meet minimum length requirements for each entry?
- ❧ respond emotionally, associatively, figuratively?
- ❧ demonstrate an accurate understanding of the literary facts of *Romeo and Juliet*?
- ❧ demonstrate an honest effort to begin making sense of the play and developing an understanding of it?
- ❧ probe responses and attempt to understand them rather than only summarize or paraphrase the action of the play?

Character Diary

As one of two on-going writing-to-learn activities that students may use during their reading of *Romeo and Juliet,* the character diary has two *instructional goals:*

- ❧ to summarize and reflect upon the meaning of the play
- ❧ to begin to evaluate the action of the play from the perspective of an individual character

Guidelines for Assessment:

Does the student

- ❧ record an entry for each reading session?
- ❧ meet minimum length requirements for each entry?
- ❧ provide an account of how the character learns of the action of the scene(s) just read?
- ❧ demonstrate an accurate understanding of the literary facts of *Romeo and Juliet?*
- ❧ demonstrate an honest effort to begin making sense of the play and developing an understanding of it?
- ❧ probe responses and attempt to understand them rather than only summarize or paraphrase the action of the play?

Viewing a Scene on Videotape

Unlike using a scene to introduce *Romeo and Juliet*, viewing a scene after students have read it provides additional information that may help them to understand the text of the play.

Instructional Goals:

- ❧ to recognize that the performance of a scene affects the student's understanding, comprehension, and interpretation of it
- ❧ to compare and contrast a student's interpretation of a scene with the performers'

Guidelines for Assessment:

Does the student

- ❧ attempt to answer all the questions?
- ❧ address the issues in the questions?
- ❧ demonstrate an honest effort to make sense of the presentation?
- ❧ begin to make connections between the videotaped presentation and the text of *Romeo and Juliet*?

Guides to Character Development

Although students complete these activities after they've read each act, they will reread and contemplate specific portions of the play actively. The students may examine Romeo and Juliet as major characters and Mercutio and the Nurse as minor ones.

Instructional Goals:

- ❧ to recognize and identify means that Shakespeare uses to develop or reveal character
- ❧ to use evidence from the play to develop and support an interpretation of a character

Guidelines for Assessment:

Does the student

- ❧ attempt to answer all the questions?
- ❧ address the issues in the questions?
- ❧ use information from the play to develop and support logical conclusions about character(s)?

Comprehension Checks

Both the Comprehension Check and the Small Group Discussion Questions provide means for assessing each student's reading comprehension.

Comprehension Checks (multiple choice)

Instructional Goal:

- ಏ to assess reading comprehension of an entire act through factual, interpretative, and evaluative questions

Guideline for Assessment:

- ಏ answer keys appear in Appendix C

Small Group Discussion Questions

Instructional Goal:

- ಏ to assess reading comprehension of an entire act through factual, interpretative, and evaluative questions

Guidelines for Assessment:

Does the student

- ಏ participate in discussion?
- ಏ attempt to answer all the questions?
- ಏ address the issues in the questions?
- ಏ use information from the play to develop and support logical conclusions about the play?

Critical Thinking Questions

Instructional Goals:

- ಏ to connect the play to the student's life in meaningful ways
- ಏ to evaluate interpretations of the play using textual evidence, personal experience, and knowledge of related literature

Guidelines for Assessment:

Does the student

- ಏ attempt to answer both the exploration questions as well as the focus question?
- ಏ address the issues of each question appropriately?
- ಏ use specific information to support ideas?
- ಏ integrate personal experience, knowledge of related literature, and textual evidence?

ᴀ draw logical conclusions from the existing evidence?

Language Exploration Activities

Instructional Goals:

> ᴀ to review definitions of selected literary devices and examine them within the context of *Romeo and Juliet*
>
> ᴀ to apply knowledge of literary devices with textual evidence to develop and evaluate interpretations of specific passages of *Romeo and Juliet*

Guidelines for Assessment:

> Suggested answers appear in Appendix C.
> Does the student
>
> ᴀ complete the items that the teacher assigns?
>
> ᴀ make an effort to apply the definition of the literary device to the lines in the play?
>
> ᴀ review the passage within the broader context of the individual speech, scene, or play?
>
> ᴀ provide specific support of interpretation(s)?

Language Exploration Review Quiz

Instructional Goal:

> ᴀ to assess the student's understanding of how specific literary devices affect the interpretation of specific passages from *Romeo and Juliet*

Guidelines for Assessment:

> An answer key appears in Appendix C.
> Has the student
>
> ᴀ completed the preceding language exploration activities?

Vocabulary in Context

Instructional Goals:

> ᴀ to review the additional meanings of words
>
> ᴀ to analyze the use of specific words within the context of a particular passage
>
> ᴀ to develop interpretations of specific passages using knowledge and context

Guidelines for Assessment:

> Suggested answers appear in Appendix C.
> Does the student

❦ complete the items that the teacher assigns?

❦ review the definitions of the words?

❦ make an effort to apply the meaning of the word to the lines in the play?

❦ review the passage within the broader context of the individual speech, scene, or play?

❦ provide specific support of interpretation(s)?

Vocabulary Review Quizzes

Instructional Goal:

❦ to assess student's understanding of specific words in context

Guidelines for Assessment:

Suggested answers appear in Appendix C.
Has the student

❦ reviewed the meaning of the words?

❦ completed the preceding vocabulary in context activities?

Individual or Group Extending Activities

Instructional Goals:

❦ to apply knowledge and understanding of *Romeo and Juliet* to new situations and contexts

❦ to provide additional opportunities for students to apply reading, writing, speaking, listening, viewing, and critical thinking skills

Guidelines for Assessment:

Does the student

❦ have a purpose and focus for the extending activity that is related to the play and the study of it directly?

❦ present information clearly and logically?

❦ present information, whether from the play or research, accurately and with appropriate documentation?

❦ present interpretations of characters or events from the play that are consistent with the information in the text?

❦ meet all appropriate additional criteria and specifications that the teacher sets?

Appendix B

USING SMALL GROUPS SUCCESSFULLY

I advocate using small groups throughout this resource. Small groups are a great way to get lots of students involved quickly. Several practices make these groups operate more effectively:

- Assign students to specific groups. When they self-select their groups, they may socialize rather than focus on the tasks at hand.

- Mix students of different backgrounds, abilities, and talents. In discussion situations, multiple perspectives often lead to insights.

- Structure the group assignments and provide written directions (on the chalkboard, overhead projector, or in written handouts). When students know their audience and the purpose of the assignment, they tend to stay on task. All members of the group need to understand what their jobs are, what the final product needs to look like, and how much time they have to complete it.

- Establish class rules for small group behavior and encourage students to work together.

- Monitor students' behavior as they work in groups. Move around the room in random fashion.

Appendix C

ANSWER KEYS

COMPREHENSION CHECKS

Act I		Act II		Act III	
1.	C	1.	D	1.	C
2.	B	2.	B	2.	E
3.	D	3.	E	3.	B
4.	A	4.	B	4.	B
5.	D	5.	B	5.	C

Act IV		Act V	
1.	C	1.	D
2.	D	2.	B
3.	A	3.	A
4.	B	4.	B
5.	D	5.	E

DISCUSSION QUESTIONS
FOR CHECKING COMPREHENSION

Act I

1. The Prince threatens to take the lives of Lords Montague and Capulet if the peace is broken again. In lines 92–93 of scene i, the Prince addresses Montague and Capulet.

❧

If ever you disturb our streets again,
Your lives shall pay forfeit of the peace.

❧

2. In scene ii, Romeo and his friends learn that Rosaline is among the guests when Capulet's illiterate servant asks their help reading the names on the guest list.

3. The lines suggest that Capulet will agree to Juliet marrying someone whom she chooses to marry.

4. The lines suggest that Romeo is both upset that he's fallen in love with his enemy but is accepting of his fate.

5. Romeo's speech in scene iv foreshadows the end of the play. At the end of Act I the Nurse has told both Romeo and Juliet the other's name. Both lovers recognize the danger in loving their enemy but they also accept it. In Act I, the Prince has threatened death if the families feud again, and Tybalt has shown his anger at Romeo and his friends for crashing the Capulets' party. Romeo's fears seem justified.

Act II

1. Juliet promises to send someone to him the next day to find out his wedding plans.

2. Friar Laurence has two reactions. He is first angry at Romeo for falling in and out of love so easily. His second reaction is that he hopes Romeo and Juliet's love for each other will bring a peaceful end to the feud.

3. Juliet doesn't want Romeo to swear by the moon because the moon changes phases during its monthly orbit. She wants Romeo to swear by something that she can count upon to be true, himself.

4. At first the Nurse wants to tell Juliet the whole story about the meeting with Romeo, recounting her aches and pains. When Juliet presses the Nurse for an answer, the Nurse tells Juliet about the wedding in Friar Laurence's cell only after the Nurse knows that Lady Capulet is safely in the house and that they are alone.

5. In Act II, Romeo and Juliet swear their undying love for each other in the balcony scene. Romeo goes and successfully gets Friar Laurence to consent to marry them. Romeo does meet the Nurse and tells her of the arrangements that he's made for their wedding. The final scene in the act is the wedding. All of these events suggest that Romeo and Juliet have succeeded in being happy.

Act III

1. The Prince exiles Romeo.

2. Juliet's family mistakes the tears that Juliet shed for her husband's exile as tears of grief for the death of her cousin Tybalt.

3. Mercutio means that his wound is enough to kill him. The wound is large enough to cause him to be carried into the church as a corpse and be buried in a grave subsequently.

4. Juliet's family interprets her mention of marrying Romeo as an outright refusal. Although Juliet does refuse to marry Paris, she also suggests that when she marries, it will be to admit her marriage to Romeo publicly.

5. The Nurse suggests that Juliet go ahead and marry Paris. The Nurse's logic is simple. Romeo is banished, so he can't challenge the marriage nor is there anyone who will reveal that Juliet is already married. The Nurse also sees Paris as a better match than Romeo, who is as good as dead already. Juliet sees it a greater sin to betray Romeo than to marry Paris. She resolves to go to see Friar Laurence, not to be absolved of sin but to seek solution to the problem.

Act IV

1. Friar Laurence gives Juliet a potion that will make her appear dead for forty-two hours. When her family comes to awaken her for her wedding on Thursday, they will find her dead and place her in the family tomb. In the meantime, Friar Laurence will send a letter to Romeo to come at sunset on Friday to the tomb, meet Juliet when she awakens and take her to Mantua until the friar can persuade the Prince to let them both return.

2. Capulet thinks that Friar Laurence has counseled Juliet to accept the will of her father.

3. When Paris speaks of their coming marriage, Juliet does not answer directly. Instead her answers seem to be replies to Paris, when in fact they are equally applicable to her marriage to Romeo.

4. Juliet lays out the dagger just in case the potion doesn't work and she awakens the next morning and might have to marry Paris. If the potion doesn't make her appear dead, she plans to commit suicide with the dagger.

5. The plan is too complex to succeed. Juliet considers many of the problems in scene iii before she drinks the potion: The potion may not work and Juliet could be poisoned. She could awaken in the tomb and not be rescued. Romeo may not get the message to come, or he may come too late.

Act V

1. Romeo prepares to join Juliet in death. He stops at the Apothecary and purchases poison.

2. When Brother John got to Mantua, he contacted another brother who had been visiting the sick. The officials thought that they might be infected and would not let them in.

3. Paris, who has come to Juliet's tomb to mourn, thinks that Romeo has come to vandalize the Capulet tomb out of revenge for being exiled.

4. She is angered because Romeo has taken poison, as a quick and painless means of suicide and left her with slower, more painful means.

5. As the Prince points out, all have already been punished enough. Both Montague and Capulet have lost their only children. Both families recognize the foolishness of their quarrel and vow to set up golden statues to remind the city of Romeo and Juliet.

LANGUAGE EXPLORATION ACTIVITIES

Act I: Changed Word Order

1. And those so early made are marred too soon.

2. The fair Rosaline sups at this ancient feast of Capulet's.

3. She shall be fourteen come Lammas Eve at night.

4. And sometime(s) she comes with a tithe-pig's tail.

5. And then he dreams of cutting foreign throats.

6. Then he dreams of smelling out a suit.

7. I swear she hath corns.

8. So a snowy dove trooping with doves shows
   As yonder lady o'er her fellow shows.

9. Then my lips have the sin that they have took.

10. I hold it not a sin to strike him dead.

Act II: Simile

1. The brightness of Juliet's cheek if she had stars for eyes would be brighter than daylight.

2. Juliet is compared to an angel, and she is more glorious to Romeo than any angel.

3. Romeo's name is compared to a rose's name, and, indirectly, Romeo is compared to a rose.

4. The contract is Juliet and Romeo's promises of eternal love for one another. Juliet compares their exchange of love as being as quick as lightning.

5. Juliet's love is as deep and boundless as the sea. It is unmeasurable.

6. Lovers' speech is compared to sweet music. Suggests that lovers will either say or believe anything.

7. The wanton is a spoiled child. Juliet compares Romeo to a pet bird on a short leash. The bird is allowed to hop a short distance from the owner only to be pulled back like a prisoner in chains.

8. The darkness that vanishes with the dawn is compared to a drunk.

9. Juliet complains about the Nurse's age. To Juliet, old people move as if they were dead.

10. The Nurse's head is compared to something breakable, perhaps an earthenware pot.

Act III: Metaphor

1. Night is compared to an older woman dressed in black.

2. Romeo's face (brow) is a throne where honor sits. Juliet suggests that Romeo will honor his promise to marry her.

3. Juliet's tears flow like water from a stream. Juliet suggests that she will not cry endlessly.

4. Romeo sees banishment as torment and living with Juliet in Verona as heaven.

5. Romeo compares flies to free men. His comparison suggests that even the flies are free to see and touch Juliet while he cannot once he is banished.

6. Friar Laurence compares philosophy to a knight's armor. He suggests that philosophy should help protect Romeo from the harm of banishment.

7. Friar Laurence compares the law to a friend. He reminds Romeo that the Prince had originally threatened death to anyone fighting in the streets again.

8. The lark is the servant that announces the morning with its song.

9. The streaks of sunlight through the clouds poke through like laces. The metaphor also suggests that the clouds look like lace.

10. Juliet's tears ebb and flow (start and stop) like the tides.

Act IV: Personification

1. The sun, acting as a servant, draws back curtains from Aurora's (goddess of the dawn) bed.

2. April steps upon the heels of Winter. April is pushing Winter out of the way.

3. Romeo urges the sun (Juliet) to kill the moon who is jealous.

4. Juliet is bound to her father until she marries. Here, bondage cannot speak because it's hoarse.

5. Morning smiles while night frowns. Morning is bright and cheery.

6. Happiness is well dressed (best array) and greets Romeo.

7. The rising sun seems to stand on tiptoe like a child looking over a wall or windowsill.

8. Death has married Juliet and become the heir to Capulet's fortune rather than Juliet or her children.

9. Time looks upon the events of the past hour.

10. Human nature makes people grieve; rationally, however, people can find joy in death.

Act V: Apostrophe

1. Mercutio makes fun of the absent Romeo for being in love.

2. Romeo speaks to Juliet whom he is afraid to speak to directly.

3. Juliet addresses Romeo and contemplates that his name rather than Romeo is her enemy.

4. Romeo addresses Juliet. He feels that loving her has made him less brave.

5. The Nurse grieves for Tybalt.

6. Juliet speaks to Romeo who is in exile. She defends his name and honor.

7. Juliet addresses Fortune or Fate. She comments upon the irony of her situation.

8. Capulet speaks to Juliet who he believes is dead.

9. Romeo speaks to the stars that he believes control his fate. He states that he will take charge of his own fate.

10. Romeo speaks to Juliet whom he believes is dead. He pledges to kill himself to join her in death.

LANGUAGE EXPLORATION REVIEW

1.	D
2.	D
3.	C
4.	C
5.	D
6.	D
7.	B
8.	A
9.	A
10.	D

VOCABULARY IN CONTEXT

With all these exercises, encourage students to discuss their ideas and interpretations, for their answers will vary. These are suggestions and shouldn't be interpreted as the only valid responses.

Act I

1. The lines suggest that Romeo's sadness produces tears that increase or intensify the wetness of the ground covered with dew.

2. Here, Benvolio uses adversary to mean *foe* or *enemy*.

3. *Chastity* as a noun, describes the state of Rosaline's overall behavior as modest, pure, decent, not just that she is a virgin.

4. Romeo finds Rosaline's eyes to be especially beautiful and charming.

5. The Prince lets everyone know that the penalty for another fight will be death. Similarly, Romeo, too, speaks of a penalty of early death.

6. Benvolio wants to know the nature of Romeo's problem.

7. The Prince, who is fed up with recurring violence, sees the fighting as destructive and potentially lethal.

8. The Nurse is extremely sure of the truth, which she states with conviction.

9. Given the religious imagery of the scene between Romeo and Juliet, Romeo would have the sin of her kiss absolved or forgiven.

10. Tybalt refers to the formality and dignity of the banquet because both the Prince and his cousin, Paris, are attending.

Act II

1. Mercutio is calling upon the spirit of Rosaline, with whom he believes Romeo has fallen in love and has run away to find, to make Romeo reappear magically. Mercutio equates falling in love with falling under a magical spell.

2. Romeo is exaggerating the brightness of Juliet's beauty. It is so great that the moon should be jealous of its brilliance.

3. Romeo sees Juliet's reaction to danger or fear when he looks at her.

4. Juliet, although being playful, is talking about playing the part of being contrary or deliberately cross.

5. Juliet works to convince the Nurse to meet Romeo and find out about the marriage plans.

6. In these lines, both the archaic past tense form *chid(e)st* and *chide* convey a sense of scolding.

7. Friar Laurence feels that Romeo must either be bothered by something or be ill to be up so early.

8. Romeo's act of pleading of the Friar is done so that he can convince him to perform the marriage. Romeo feels that marrying Juliet will benefit both families.

9. Juliet is referring to the lies that lovers swear to each other.

10. Juliet speaks of the messengers of love.

Act III

1. Benvolio comments upon the Capulets, especially Tybalt, prowling the streets looking for Romeo.

2. In this rather unusual use of *discover*, Benvolio offers to reveal how the fight began.

3. The Prince punishes Romeo by expelling him from Verona. Romeo must leave and never return upon threat of death.

4. Romeo has been expelled from the city-state of Verona by order of the Prince.

5. Here Juliet treats Romeo's name as his character which she recognizes she has marred badly.

6. *Naught* works two ways here: to characterize all men as wicked, as well as "good for nothing."

7. Tributary, along with the reference to a spring, suggests that Juliet's tears have come in a steady stream.

8. Here *purgatory* is equated with hell rather than as a place of temporary torment.

9. Juliet, treating fortune as a person, asks that Fortune change her mind and end Romeo's exile, returning him to her.

10. Juliet comments that her mother is up at an unusual hour; either something has kept Lady Capulet up late or caused her to arise early.

Act IV

1. The friar has asked sincerely for the time to meet with Juliet alone. Paris thinks the friar will hear confession while the audience knows that Friar Laurence and Juliet will discuss an escape plan.

2. Paris comments on Juliet's excessive weeping, presuming that she grieves for Tybalt rather than being separated from her husband.

3. Juliet probably appears both thoughtful and sad.

4. Friar Laurence realizes that Juliet is not going to be allowed to put off or postpone the marriage to Paris.

5. Juliet suggests that ghosts of the dead relatives are thought to come out and play.

6. *Waned ashes* would be the grayish white ones that are cold. In other words she will have the pale color, or lack of color, of a dead person.

7. Lord Capulet, because he's planning his only daughter's wedding feast, is looking for especially skillful cooks.

8. Juliet is suggesting that she throw herself at her father's feet and ask his forgiveness.

9. Juliet has selected her best clothes for the ceremony tomorrow.

10. Juliet fears being smothered in the vault by breathing only the bad smelling air.

Act V

1. Balthasar saw Juliet laid in the family tomb.

2. Romeo sees the world as a disgusting place.

3. Romeo hopes that his dreams foretell good news.

4. Romeo plans to meet Balthasar directly.

5. Friar John sought out another member of the same religious order to help him find Romeo.

6. *Pestilence* here means any deadly disease.

7. The Page is willing to take a risk.

8. Romeo wants Balthasar to remain detached or immobile and ignore any sounds that the servant might hear.

9. Paris sees Romeo as proud and arrogant, for Paris knows that Romeo is defying the Prince's orders to be back in Verona.

10. In this passage, Juliet wants to die so she can restore her marriage to Romeo.

VOCABULARY REVIEW QUIZZES

Act I		Act II		Act III		Act IV		Act V	
1.	C	1.	C	1.	B	1.	B	1.	C
2.	D	2.	B	2.	B	2.	C	2.	A
3.	C	3.	A	3.	D	3.	A	3.	B
4.	A	4.	D	4.	A	4.	A	4.	B
5.	B	5.	D	5.	D	5.	D	5.	D
6.	B	6.	B	6.	C	6.	B	6.	C
7.	C	7.	D	7.	D	7.	A	7.	D
8.	A	8.	C	8.	A	8.	D	8.	B
9.	D	9.	A	9.	B	9.	C	9.	B
10.	C	10.	D	10.	D	10.	A	10.	A

Appendix D

BIBLIOGRAPHY

Abcarian, Richard and Marvin Klotz, eds. *Literature: The Human Experience*. rev., shorter ed. New York: St. Martin's, 1984.

Allen, Grant and George C. Williamson. *Cities of Northern Italy: Verona, Padua, Bologna, and Ravenna*. Vol. 2. Boston: L. C. Page, 1906.

Barnet, Sylvan, Morton Berman, and William Burto, eds. *An Introduction to Literature: Fiction, Poetry, Drama*. Glenview: Scott, Foresman, 1989.

Bleich, David. *Readings and Feelings: A Guide to Subjective Criticism*. Urbana: National Council of Teachers of English, 1975.

Brockett, Oscar G. *History of the Theater*. Boston: Allyn and Bacon, 1968.

Brown, Hazel and Brian Cambourne. *Read and Retell: A Strategy for the Whole-Language / Natural Learning Classroom*. Portsmouth: Heinemann, 1987.

Cambourne, Brian. *The Whole Story: Natural Learning and the Acquisition of Literacy in the Classroom*. New York: Ashton-Scholastic, 1989.

Christenbury, Leila and Patricia P. Kelly. *Questioning: A Path to Critical Thinking*. ERIC/RCS Theory and Research into Practice (TRIP) Monograph Series. Urbana: NCTE, 1983.

Fox, Levi. *William Shakespeare: A Concise Life*. Norwich, England: Jerrold Printing, 1991.

Hammond Atlas of World History. Maplewood: Hammond, 1968.

Lee, Charlotte and David Grote. *Theater: Preparation and Performance*. Glenview: Scott, Foresman, 1982.

Miller, Bruce E. *Teaching the Art of Literature*. Urbana: National Council of Teachers of English, 1980.

Mizner, Arthur, ed. *Teaching Shakespeare: A Guide to the Teaching of Macbeth, Julius Caesar, The Merchant of Venice, Hamlet, Romeo and Juliet, A Midsummer Night's Dream, Othello, As You Like It, Twelfth Night, Richard II, Henry IV, Part One, The Tempest*. New York: The New American Library, Inc., 1969.

Muir, Ramsey. *Muir's Atlas of Ancient & Classical History*. 2nd. ed. New York: Barnes and Noble Inc., 1956.

Robinson, Randal. *Unlocking Shakespeare's Language*. ERIC/RCS Theory and Research into Practice (TRIP) Monograph Series. Urbana: NCTE, 1989.

Romeo and Juliet in *William Shakespeare: The Complete Works*. Charles Jasper Sisson, ed. New York: Harper & Row, 1953: 879–909.

Stanford, Judith A. *Responding to Literature*. Mountain View: Mayfield Publishing, 1992.

Vaughn, Joseph L. and Thomas H. Estes. *Reading and Reasoning Beyond the Primary Grades*. Boston: Allyn and Bacon, 1986.

Willek, Rene and Austin Warren. *Theory of Literature*. 3rd ed. New York: Harcourt, Brace & World, Inc., 1970.

Appendix E

VERSIONS OF *ROMEO AND JULIET* AVAILABLE ON VIDEOTAPE

Romeo and Juliet. (1936). Leslie Howard and Norma Shearer. Black and White. 126 minutes.

Romeo and Juliet. (1954). Laurence Harvey and Susan Shentall. Color. 135 minutes.

Romeo and Juliet. (1968). Directed by Franco Zeffirelli with Olivia Hussey, Leonard Whiting, and Michael York. Color. 138 minutes.

Romeo and Juliet. (1979). BBC/PBS production for "Shakespeare's Plays" series. Sir John Gielgud, Rebecca Saire, Patrick Ryecart. Color. 167 minutes.

Availability and Cost:

The Zeffirelli and BBC/PBS versions are available generally through larger video rental chains, state or regional public libraries, or state or regional educational film/media service libraries. Check with your school's librarian or media specialist.

Costs to purchase these video versions range from $25–$100.

The Writing Company issues a special Shakespeare Catalog. Address: 10200 Jefferson Boulevard, Culver City, CA 90232.

All versions listed above are available at present from Filmic Archives, The Cinema Center, Botsford, CT 06404. 1–800–366–1920.